The Epistles of Paul the Apostle

The• Epistles of Paul the Apostle

A Sketch of Their Origin and Contents

George Findlay

AMG
PUBLISHERS

Chattanooga, TN 37421

The Epistles of Paul the Apostle

A SKETCH OF THEIR ORIGIN AND CONTENTS

The 4th edition originally published by
Robert Culley, London.

ISBN 0–89957–244-8

Library of Congress Catalog Card Number: 98–85087

Printed in the United States of America
03 02 01 00 99 98 –R– 6 5 4 3 2 1

To My Students,
Past and Present,
For Whom the Lectures Embodied in
This Little Volume Were Prepared

Contents

Foreword

It is a great pleasure to present George G. Findlay's book *The Epistles of Paul the Apostle*. Because of Findlay's many years of study as both a student and educator of Paul's Epistles, we can greatly benefit from his work. His study is uniquely focused not on Paul the writer so much as on his writings. *The Epistles of Paul the Apostle* concentrates on the works of Paul while telling the story of his journeys to preach Jesus Christ to the churches in the areas of the world of his day. As we learn about the struggles of the churches to which he writes, we also learn how to deal with the struggles we face in our churches and individually today.

Each chapter ends with Findlay's paraphrases of significant passages. Charts within the pages of each chapter are also helpful summaries of the events of each epistle. The map located on the inside back cover will help the reader visualize the movements of the letters, where they were written and where they were delivered.

In creating this volume, we at AMG Publishers have made a few minor changes to the original work to help clarify its content for modern readers by updating spelling according to the change of our language over the years, and in some cases, by simplifying unusual forms of punctuation. We have also added some Scripture references to help the reader more readily find quoted passages. However, Findlay's original meaning has not been changed in any way, and his insightful studies of Paul's epistles have been preserved for generations to come.

Preface

Why another book about Paul? We have Commentaries, Lives, and Introductions to the great apostle in abundance. This book comes under none of these designations, and it fills a place that, so far as the writer knows, is unoccupied. It seeks to weave the Epistles together into a historical unity, to trace the life that pervades them, alike in its internal elements and external movements and surroundings, and to do this in a volume of small compass, and free from technical detail and phraseology.

Bibliographical references and extended critical discussions are excluded by the limits of the work. Conclusions must be given, where reasons are unsupplied or only hinted, and conjecture has often to supply the lack of sure knowledge. The writer has striven to assert nothing more strongly than the evidence warrants. But it is difficult to be brief and yet not too positive.

These pages may claim, at any rate, to be the outcome of many years of constant study and teaching devoted to the subject.

George G. Findlay
(1892)

This work has been revised throughout for the THIRD EDITION. Some additions have been made to it, including a Postscript upon *The Locality of Paul's Galatia,* occasioned by the "South Galatian theory" of Professor W. M. Ramsay, who in his able and brilliant work on *The Church in the Roman Empire* identifies the "Galatians" of the epistle with the churches of Pisidian Antioch, Iconium, Lystra, and Derbe. An improved map is also given on the inside back cover.

For the preparation of the Index I am indebted to my friend the Rev. C. F. Hunter, B.A.

In the Fourth Edition several important Notes have been inserted, and the Chronology amended in the light of later research.

Introduction

It is the object of this handbook to furnish, in a form as brief and clear as possible, a connected view of the epistles of Paul. We shall look at them in their historical order and continuity, as an expression of the living mind of the great apostle of the Gentiles and a part of his life-work. We shall seek to understand their environment, the combination of circumstances under which they originated and the condition of the young Christian communities to which they were addressed. We shall treat the letters as an organic whole, viewing each in its relation to its companions and to the general teaching of the author, and endeavoring to trace out their internal unity and pervasive spirit. We shall follow the progress of the writer's thought, and the application of his governing principles to the changing conditions of life around him, and to the growing necessities of the work of God committed to his charge. These epistles will afford us, if we succeed in our attempt, a mirror of the apostle himself in his inner history and experience, in the varying moods of his sensitive and ardent nature, in the advance of his powerful intellect and the mighty working of the Spirit of Christ upon him; a mirror also, on the other hand, of the state and development of the infant churches of the Gentiles which he had begotten, and nursed through the early and imperiled stages of their existence.

At the same time, while keeping these wider aims before us, the letters themselves will be our proper study. Our chief object will be to grasp and master each of them in its special significance and character, as in turn they come under review. It will be possible, as we hope, without entering upon the details of exposition, to analyze the Epistles in such a way as to bring out their salient features and distinctive import, so that we may appreciate each for its own sake, and may discern what they severally contribute to Christian doctrine and to the wealth and life of the church, as well as to our acquaintance with Paul and the apostolic age. If we accomplish less than we design and our ambition should prove too large to be compassed in so small a space, the reader must be pleased to accept what is here offered him as an essay towards the end proposed, and as the opening up of a path which it will remain for himself to pursue to its goal. It is something if this sketch suffices to indicate to the student the method by which the subject should be approached and the ideal that he must place before himself, even though the results immediately attained fall short of its realization.

The path which we have marked out is indeed no new or untrodden way. We are entering into the labors of many devoted Pauline scholars. The life and writings of this apostle have engaged of recent years the attention and research of men of all schools of Christian learning, to an extraordinary degree. The work thus accomplished is so far complete and the material accumulated for the elucidation of the subject so extensive and well-digested, that little remains to be done except to gather up and bring to a focus the results now ascertained. It ought not, therefore, to be very difficult for us, within these narrow limits, to take such a rapid but comprehensive survey of the field as we have above indicated.

In the two opening chapters we shall aim at two things. (1) We shall draw out *a chronological outline of the apostle's life* supplying a framework into which to fit the Epistles provisionally, so that each may have its definite place in our mental image of the times. For in compositions of this class, more than in any other, a preliminary knowledge of the occasion and date of writing is indispensable for the understanding of their contents.[1] Furnishing ourselves beforehand with a scheme of the apostle's history, gathered from a cursory view of the Epistles and comparison of them with Acts, we shall return to the closer study of the letters, prepared to trace the course of events that gave birth to each, the links of connection which bind them together, and the nature and extent of their various contributions to the teaching of the New Testament. (2) Furthermore, and as our second preliminary business, we shall take account of *the literary form and characteristics of Paul's letters*, their peculiar style of expression and the mold into which they are cast.

George G. Findlay
(ca. 1892)

---

1. In following Paul's career, we need also to have the map constantly before us (see the inside back cover). W. M. Ramsay's Paul the Traveler and the Roman Citizen illuminates this subject on many sides.

The Chronology of
Paul's Life

The apostle's *conversion to Christianity* is variously dated by different critics, some fixing it as early as A.D. 35, others as late as A.D. 41. Its date is determined: (1) partly by its connection with Stephen's martyrdom which, it is supposed, took place about the end of Pontius Pilate's governorship (A.D. 36), when his authority was so weak that such a proceeding as the judicial murder of Stephen becomes accountable or in the interregnum that preceded the arrival of Pilate's successor (A.D. 36–38); (2) partly by counting backwards from the date of the council at Jerusalem (on the assumption that the meeting of Acts 15:1–29 and that of Gal. 2:1–10 are one and the same) the fourteen years[1] of Galatians 2:1 (including, probably, the three of Gal. 1:18), and the council appears on other grounds to have taken place in A.D. 49; and (3) partly again by reference to 2 Corinthians 11:32, where Paul tells us that *Aretas*, king of Petra in Arabia, was *occupying Damascus* at the time of his escape from that city, which ensued

---

1. It must be borne in mind that ancient computations of time were *inclusive*, the starting point and the terminus of the period computed being both reckoned in counting the distance. So that, *for example*, any event of the year 38 would be described as "three years after" any event of the year 36, although the former should have occurred in October and the latter in September. (The Jewish civil year began in October.) At this rate, it is evident that the two associated periods of fourteen and three years, stated by Paul, need not have amounted to more than actual intervals of twelve years and one respectively.

on his return there (Acts 9:23–25) after his retreat and sojourn in Arabia (Gal. 1:17, 18). Now Aretas, it is shown, cannot have occupied Damascus earlier than A.D. 37 (when the death of the Emperor Tiberius was attended with considerable unsettlement in the eastern parts of the Empire), and the Arab chief does not appear to have held that city at the time of Saul's previous journey there.

These data taken singly seem precarious, but they lend confirmation to each other, and we infer from them that the conversion of Saul of Tarsus to the faith of Jesus Christ took place in the year 36 of our Lord. It may have come about a year sooner or a year later, but the margin of uncertainty can hardly extend beyond this limit. It was, then, within six, or at the most seven years of Christ's ascension that this great event happened, when the ascended Jesus led captive this powerful and determined enemy of His name, and through him bestowed upon men gifts among the choicest and most fruitful with which His church has ever been enriched. In Paul's conversion the full import of the new faith revealed itself; a worldwide revolution was effected in the germ.

Referring the conversion of Saul to the year 36, his *first* subsequent *visit to Jerusalem* took place in A.D. 38 (Acts 9:26–30; Gal. 1:18, 19), when he "went up . . . to see Peter, and abode with him fifteen days," and also "saw . . . James, the Lord's brother," but did not become known to the Judean church at large (Gal. 1:22), though he "argued" in the Hellenistic synagogues. After this the future apostle retired to Tarsus, and spent some years engaged in evangelistic work in "the regions of Syria and Cilicia," near to his native place (Gal. 1:21–23).

First Period of Paul's Public Ministry

He reappears in the narrative of Acts, when fetched by Barnabas to help him at Antioch (Acts 11:25, 26). This must have been in A.D. 43, for Barnabas and Saul labored in Antioch together "an entire year" before the prediction by Agabus of the famine in Judea. This calamity occasioned their going up to Jerusalem, during the persecution of the church there by Herod Agrippa I, which was terminated by the sudden death of this king (Acts 12). Now at this point in our chronology we touch solid ground, for we know from secular history that Herod died at Caesarea in April A.D. 44 At this period Paul made his *second visit* as a Christian to Jerusalem, assisting Barnabas in bringing relief to the famine-stricken brethren in Judea (Acts 11:27–30; 12:25).

This was probably a hurried and secret visit: it was "to the elders" that the contribution from Antioch was officially sent, and coming at such a time, with a contribution of money for the proscribed Christian flock, the delegates would avoid public notice. It is likely that Paul saw hardly anyone at Jerusalem except the elders, for Peter was at this time in hiding (Acts 12:17) or still confined in prison, and the other apostles probably absent. Indeed, it is quite possible that Paul did not even set foot in the city. At any rate, he still remained "unknown by sight to the churches of Judea" (Gal. 1:22). This errand had no bearing on Paul's relations to the other apostles, and was irrelevant to his purpose in Galatians 1 and 2. Hence he passes it over without mention in that epistle. He refers there to two important visits to the Holy City, which brought him into close relations with Peter and the leaders of the mother church: the first taking place in the third year after his conversion, which we have noticed in its place and a second following the conversion "after an interval of fourteen years," when the status of Gentile Christians and of Paul as their apostle was under discussion (Gal. 2:1–10). Now, the mission of charity referred to in Acts 11:29, 30 befell in the course of this period of fourteen years, about A.D. 44.

"And Barnabas and Saul returned from Jerusalem, when they had fulfilled their mission, taking along with them John, who was also called Mark" (Acts 12:25), who was "Barnabas' cousin" (Col. 4:10). For some time longer they continued their labors in Antioch and the neighborhood, Paul's work extending beyond Syria to his native district of Cilicia (Gal. 1:21). At length came the call of the Spirit which drove the Gentile missionaries farther afield and gave the signal for the commencement of Paul's wider career (Acts 13:1–4). *The first missionary journey* of Barnabas and Paul together took them from Antioch through the island of Cyprus and the southeast of Asia Minor, and back by sea to Antioch again (Acts 13, 14). This extensive tour occupied probably the greater part of two years, from early spring to a second autumn (during winter navigation, and travel in the highlands of Asia Minor, were impracticable). But it is impossible to determine to which of the years between A.D. 44 and 49 it belonged. The language of Luke would lead us to date the expedition at an earlier rather than a later position in this interval; if we assign to it A.D. 46–47, we are not far from the truth. Luke tells us that "a long time" elapsed between the return of the missionaries from this voyage and their going up to Jerusalem on the question of Gentile circumcision (Acts 14:28).

For some time longer, therefore, the apostle Paul remained by the side of Barnabas, laying securely the foundations of Gentile Christianity in the Greco-Syrian city of Antioch, which was the metropolis of the East and at this time inferior in its magnitude and wealth only to Rome and Alexandria. If Paul spent eighteen months of his brief apostleship continuously at Corinth and above two years at Ephesus, it was not too much to devote the first five years of his public ministry to Antioch. Here "the disciples were first called Christians in Antioch" (Acts 11:26), and Antioch, rather than Jerusalem, is the mother city of Christian missions and of the church ecumenical. It was the headquarters and starting point of Paul's whole Gentile evangelism. While remaining at Antioch, the apostle probably undertook other minor expeditions in the neighboring regions, resembling that described in Acts 13, 14, but which it was not necessary for Luke to relate.

To the time of the first recorded missionary journey belong the addresses reported in Acts 13, 14, delivered at the Pisidian Antioch and at Lystra in Lycaonia, which are of great value to us as examples of Paul's missionary preaching.

The so-called "Council of Jerusalem" (Acts 15; Gal. 2) is the next critical event in the apostle's life and in the annals of the primitive church. It took place in A.D. 49, or thereabouts, at a point of time nearly halfway between the ascension of Christ and the fall of Jerusalem. This conference between Barnabas and Paul, as delegates of the church at Antioch, and the chiefs of the church at Jerusalem resulted in the formal recognition of Gentile Christianity in its distinctive character and independence of the Mosaic Law. An understanding was brought about, under the auspices of "James, Cephas, and John," between the conservative Judean school and those who shared in the more advanced and enlightened views of the apostle of the Gentiles; while the latter, in spite of the prejudices that had been excited against him, was acknowledged in his plenary apostleship by the three "pillars" at Jerusalem and admitted to a footing of equality with themselves. Thus his position with that of the new free Gentile communities was made secure, and a platform was laid for the widest possible extension of the gospel throughout the heathen world.

Second Period of Paul's Ministry

From this point, therefore, Paul's plans took a wider range and his gospel had free course. He set out on the *second missionary journey* independently of Barnabas, but accompanied by Silas (or "Silvanus," as in 1 and 2 Thess. 1:1; 1 Pet. 5:12) of Jerusalem (Acts 15:36–41), Timothy joining them at Lystra on the way (Acts 16:1–3), and Luke apparently attending them at a later period of the journey, from Troas to Philippi (Acts 16:10–17, for it is in this part of the journey that the writer of Acts speaks in the *first person pl.*). The primary object of this tour was to confirm the churches already founded in south-eastern Asia Minor, and to deliver to them the letter of the council at Jerusalem (Acts 15:36, 41; 16:4, 5). But when the missionary band had reached the limit of the former excursion, instead of returning home they boldly marched forward through the heart of the peninsula. Leaving Lycaonia to the south, they traversed "the Phrygian and Galatian region" (Acts 16:5), in a direction apparently from south to north. In Galatia the apostle's health broke down, and he was compelled to halt. Here, in all probability, he spent the winter; he was received with the kindest hospitality, and preached with great success (Gal. 3:1–5; 4:12–15). On leaving Pisidian Antioch, Paul and Silas had set out westwards, intending to attack the important Roman province of Asia, with its famous capital Ephesus. But they were "forbidden by the Holy Spirit," and a similar intimation stopped them later at the border of the populous province of Bithynia, lying far to the north (Acts 16:6, 7).

So it came to pass that in the spring of the year 50 the travelers found themselves in Troas, fronting Europe and the western seas, where the cry from Macedonia reached their ears. At its summons they crossed the Aegean, to take possession in the name of Christ of a new continent, the home of the world's imperial races, the nurse of civilization and the arts of life. The graphic narrative of Luke, in Acts 16:11—18:18, enables us to follow closely the track of the missionaries and to witness their adventures and successes from Troas all the way to Corinth. Here Paul "settled there a year and six months," and "remained many days longer" (Acts 18:11, 18, probably from fall 50 to summer 52), and this city, the political and commercial capital of Greece, became, after Antioch, the second great center of the Gentile Christian mission. The arrival of Aquila and his wife at Corinth in consequence of the expulsion of the Jews from Rome by the Emperor Claudius (Acts 18:2), and the governorship of Gallio in the province of Achaia, at this point bring the sacred narrative into contact with secular history. These coincidences, while not supplying very definite marks of time, yet, so far as they go, sustain the correctness of our chronology.

The churches of Galatia, Macedonia, and Corinth were the product of Paul's second missionary journey. And to this period belong the firstfruits of the apostle's literary labors, *the two epistles to the Thessalonians*. Add to these the address in the Areopagus (Acts 17:18–31).

Third Period of Paul's Ministry

A brief and unimportant *fourth visit to Jerusalem* is indicated in Acts 18:22, 23; after which the apostle "went down to Antioch." He "spent some time" in that city, probably the winter of A.D. 52–53, and it was, we believe, at this time, in the interval between the second and third missionary journeys, that the conflict took place at Antioch between Peter and Paul, which the latter apostle describes in Galatians 2:11–21. Our reasons for this opinion will afterwards appear, under the heading "The Conflict with Peter" in chapter 4.

Paul started from Antioch, on his *third missionary journey*, in the spring of A.D. 53. He journeyed overland, "passed successively through the Galatian region and Phrygia, strengthening all the disciples," and therefore (see the map on the inside back cover) visiting the Lyaconian churches also on his way (Acts 18:23). He was able now to carry out the purpose, postponed three years before by the divine monition which then directed his course to Europe, of coming down by way of the Phrygian highlands to Ephesus. Here he arrived (Acts 19:1) in the latter part of the year 53. And he remained in or about Ephesus for some two years and a half (cf. the notes of time given us in Acts 19:8, 10; 20:31), in which time a large and flourishing church was established in this great capital, and "all who lived in Asia heard the word of the Lord, both Jews and Greeks" (Acts 19:10). The churches of the Lycus valley, Colossae, Laodicea, and Hierapolis, where Paul himself had not been (Col. 1:5–7, 2:1), were proofs of the far-reaching influence of the apostle's Ephesian ministry, and of the abundant harvest which his labors yielded in this well-chosen soil.

The tumult in the theater at Ephesus somewhat hastened Paul's departure. He left Asia in the spring of 56, traveling, as before, by way of Troas to Macedonia (Acts 20:1; 2 Cor. 2:12). Here he must have stayed a considerable time (Acts 20:2; 2 Cor. 1:23), longer than at first he intended. It was probably during this summer that Paul completed the evangelization of Macedonia, and made the excursion into Illyricum referred to in Romans 15:19. The autumn of 56 found him in Corinth again, to which he devoted the three months of winter (Acts 20:3). Early in the year 57 Paul set out, by way of Macedonia, on the memorable voyage to Jerusalem which concluded the third and culminating period of his Gentile mission. By Easter he was already at Philippi (Acts 20:6); here Luke rejoined him, for he now resumes the "we" dropped at Philippi six years before (Acts 16:17).

To this epoch (A.D. 53–57) belong the founding of the churches of Asia (i.e., the Roman province of Asia, corresponding to western Asia Minor in modern geography), with Ephesus for their metropolis, and the writing of the Galatian, the two Corinthian, and the Roman epistles: the greatest products of the apostle's pen, and documents whose authorship is beyond fair dispute. To the year 57 and the time of the journey to Jerusalem belongs the pastoral address to the Ephesian elders recorded in Acts 20. This forms the transition to the following period.

Fourth Period of Paul's Ministry

It was Pentecost, A.D. 57 when the apostle paid his *fifth visit to Jerusalem* (Acts 20:16; 21:17), bringing with him the contributions that the Gentile churches had made for the relief of their poorer brethren in Judea (Acts 24:17; Rom. 15:25–27, 31, etc.) "The Jews from Asia" present at the feast (Acts 21:27–30), his old Ephesian enemies, recognized him in the Temple and made a murderous assault upon him, setting the whole city in an uproar. He was with difficulty rescued by Captain Claudius Lysias and the Roman guard; was tried before the Sanhedrin without result, and then dispatched for safety to Caesarea, the residence of the Procurator; tried, again ineffectually, before Felix, he was detained two years, until the expiry of Felix's governorship and the arrival of his successor Festus (A.D. 59). Failing to obtain justice from the new Procurator, he "appealed to Caesar" in the exercise of his right as a Roman citizen, and thus secured the fulfillment of his long-cherished hope of seeing Rome (Acts 19:21; Rom. 15:23). Our calculations, drawn from Luke's data, are verified at this point by certain statements of Josephus, from which we gather that Festus succeeded Felix as Procurator of Judea not earlier than the summer of 58 nor later than that of A.D. 61.

Paul's speeches of defense are important documents for this *fourth period* of his apostleship: (1) before the people, delivered from the Temple steps, Acts 22; (2) before the Jewish Sanhedrin, Acts 23; (3) before the Procurator Felix, Acts 24; (4) his appeal to Caesar at the court of Festus, Acts 25; (5) his apology before Herod Agrippa II, in the presence of Festus, Acts 26.

The voyage to Rome, narrated in the last chapters of Acts, occupied the autumn and winter of A.D. 59–60 There Luke leaves him, after "two full years" still awaiting trial. Meanwhile, he was allowed to "stay . . . in his own rented quarters, and was welcoming all who came to him; preaching the kingdom of God, and teaching concerning the Lord Jesus Christ with all openness, unhindered" (Acts 28:30, 31). So the story ends. Whatever be the real explanation of this abrupt yet seemingly designed conclusion, it is scarcely consistent with the supposition that the imprisonment terminated with the apostle's death. There was nothing in the nature of the charges against him, nor in the policy of the Roman Government, likely to lead to such an issue; unless, indeed, the Emperor had some personal ground for hostility against the Christians. Such hostility did exist, as we know, in the closing years of Nero's reign, after the great fire at Rome in A.D. 64. And tradition points to this later period as the time of the apostle's martyrdom. Moreover, the epistles to Philemon and to the Philippians, the former probably, and the latter certainly, written from Rome after Paul had been in confinement there for a considerable time, express a decided expectation of release (Phil. 2:23, 24; Phile. 22), in entire contrast to the language of 2 Timothy 4:5–8, 18.

The apostle arrived a prisoner at Rome early in the year 60, after wintering in Malta. Two years longer he remained there in military custody (Acts 28:16, 30), under the accusation of the Jews of Jerusalem. This added to the two years of detention at Caesarea, and the time occupied on the voyage, amounts to nearly five years (A.D. 57–62) out of the best part of Paul's life spent in captivity through the malice of his fellow-countrymen. This fourth period of his ministry, the time of his prison-life, was not, however, the least fruitful. To it we owe the epistles to the Ephesians, Colossians, and Philemon, with that to the Philippians.

Fifth Period of Paul's Ministry

The narrative of Luke leaves it open to us to suppose, what other historical indications lead us confidently to believe, namely, that the apostle was released from his captivity at Rome,[2] and that his ministry was prolonged to a *fifth period*, extending from A.D. 62 to 66 or 67. Of this last stage of his life the epistles to Timothy and Titus are our only memorials. For these letters it is quite impossible to find a fit place at any earlier point in Paul's history. They lie outside the field of his work as that is presented to us in Acts.

Luke's guidance having failed us, it is only in a conjectural way that we can represent to ourselves the apostle's course in these last years of his ministry. In accordance with his intention and previous custom, it is likely that on his release he made it his first business to revisit the churches already established, those of Macedonia and Asia Minor in particular (Phil. 2:24; Phile. 22). Then we can imagine him spending a happy winter once more among his old friends at Antioch (A.D. 62–63). With the spring the great apostle would set out to conquer new fields for Christ, and we are strongly inclined to think that he fulfilled his cherished purpose (Rom. 15:24) of preaching the

---

2. Harnack refers Paul's release to A.D. 59, thus finding space for the Fifth Period, including the mission to Spain, before 64, the year of the great fire of Rome and the consequent Neronian persecution, in which he supposes the apostle to have perished. But his reckoning carries back Paul's conversion to the year 30, an impossibly early date.

gospel in the far-off land of Spain, the western limit of the then known world.

How long Paul stayed in Spain, if he went there, we cannot tell. When he wrote his letter to Titus, he had recently evangelized the island of Crete, which would naturally lie on his way in the return voyage from the west (Titus 1:5). At the time of writing this epistle Paul was setting his face westwards again, intending to "winter at Nicopolis" (Titus 3:12), a port of Epirus opposite the Italian coast. The epistle to Titus is so nearly allied to the first epistle to Timothy, that it is highly probable they were composed about the same time. And the latter was addressed to Timothy at Ephesus, where the apostle had recently left him in charge, while "depart[ing] for Macedonia" (1 Tim. 1:3). The reference to Corinth in 2 Timothy 4:20 suggests that the writer on this same journey had called there also. From Macedonia or Achaia, we conjecture, these two epistles (1 Tim.; Titus) were dispatched to Ephesus and Crete respectively.

Whether the apostle ever reached his winter-quarters at Nicopolis, we know not. Second Timothy is so closely connected in thought with the other two Pastorals that it seems more likely to us that the writer was rearrested and hurried to Rome, possibly through the machinations of his enemies in Ephesus (2 Tim. 1:15; 4:14), soon after writing to his two helpers. There we find him, in the last chapter of his letter to Timothy, some time "before winter," anticipating his need of "the cloak which I left at Troas with Carpus, and the books, especially the parchments," begging "Timothy, my beloved son" to hasten to his side. He has made a first successful defense, but is nevertheless expecting, what the persecuting rage of Nero now rendered certain, that his present trial will end with his death (2 Tim. 4:16–18). "The time of my departure," he writes, "has come. I have fought the good fight, I have finished the course, I have kept the faith. . . . The Lord will deliver me from every evil deed, and will bring me safely to His heavenly kingdom; to Him be the glory forever and ever. Amen."

Tradition says that he died by beheading.

Let us now summarize our chronological results.

EVENTS OF PAUL'S LIFE	A.D.	LEADING EVENTS OF GENERAL HISTORY
Martyrdom of Stephen, and Saul's conversion.	36	Deposition of Pontius Pilate.
Saul in Arabia.	37	Death of the Emperor Tiberius, and accession of Caius (Caligula).
First visit to Jerusalem, and acquaintance with Peter, and with James, the Lord's brother.	38	Aretas in possession of Damascus.
	40	Caligula attempts to set up his statue in the Temple at Jerusalem. Deposition of Herod Antipas; suicide of Pilate.
Saul in Cilicia.	41	Death of Caius, and accession of Claudius.
		Herod Agrippa I made king of the whole of Palestine.
Saul joins Barnabas at Antioch.	43	Conquest of Britain by the Romans commenced.
Barnabas and Saul visit Jerusalem, with help against the approaching famine at the time of Herod's persecution.	44	King Herod dies; Judea placed again under a Roman Procurator.
Barnabas and Saul's expedition to Cyprus, Pisdia, and Lycaonia. *First missionary journey.*	46–7?	
Conference of Barnabas and Paul with James, Peter, and John, at Jerusalem.	48 49?	Herod Agrippa II made King of Chalcis; his power afterwards extended.

Events of Paul's Life	A.D.	Leading Events of General History
Second missionary journey, of Paul and Silas through Asia Minor, Macedonia, and Greece.	49–52 50?	Seneca made tutor to Nero (49). Jews expelled from Rome.
Epistles to the Thessalonians.	50–51 between 51 and 55	Gallio Proconsul of Achaia.
Apollos first appears at Ephesus.	52	Felix appointed Procurator of Judea.
Collision between Peter and Paul at Antioch.	Winter 52–53?	
Third missionary journey, of Paul with Timothy and Titus, through Asia Minor to Ephesus, then to Macedonia and Corinth.	53–57 54	Death of Claudius, and accession of Nero.
Riot at Ephesus. Paul's severe illness.	56	
Epistles to the Corinthians, Galatians, and Romans.	56–57 57	Jonathan, the high priest, assassinated by the *Sicarii* (Dagger-men).
Voyage to Jerusalem, arrest, and imprisonment at Caesarea.	57	
	59?	Festus made Procurator.
Appeal to Caesar.	59 Winter	Nero kills his mother Agrippina.
Voyage to Rome.	59–60 61	Revolt of Boadicea in Britain.
Two years of captivity in Rome: Epistles to the Colossians and	60–62 62?	Martyrdom of James at Jerusalem.

EVENTS OF PAUL'S LIFE	A.D.	LEADING EVENTS OF GENERAL HISTORY
PHILEMON AND EPHESIANS, also PHILIPPIANS.	62	Albinus Procurator of Judea.
Fourth missionary jour-	62–64?	
ney. Churches of Asia Minor, Macedonia and Greece revisited; Spain	64	Great fire of Rome, July 19–25; horrible persecution of Christians.
(?) and Crete evangelized.	64	Gessius Florus Procurator.
	65	Murder of Seneca by Nero.
EPISTLES TO TIMOTHY AND TITUS.	66?	Nero in Greece.
	66	Outbreak of the Jewish war against Rome.
Martyrdom of Paul.	66 or 67?	
	68	Assassination of Nero.
	68, 69	Civil war in the Empire.
	70	Fall of Jerusalem.

It will be seen that we divide the Epistles into *four* groups:

First. The two to the Thessalonians, written in the years A.D. 50–51

Second. First Corinthians, 2 Corinthians, Galatians, and Romans, written probably in this order, between the spring of A.D. 56 and of 57.

Third. Colossians, Philemon, and Ephesians, written contemporaneously, and Philippians after some interval, from Rome, probably in the year 62.

Fourth. The three Pastoral epistles: 1 Timothy, Titus, 2 Timothy, following in close succession in the last year of the apostle's life, that is, as nearly as we can judge, in A.D. 66.

The composition of the thirteen letters extended over some sixteen years, and the four groups appear to have been separated by similar intervals of time.

The *epistle to the Hebrews* does not appear in the above scheme. It does not bear Paul's name, and it is difficult to believe that it is his composition. We shall add a supplementary chapter on this epistle.

Additional Note: For discussion of the Chronology of Paul's life, and on other topics calling for further inquiry, the writer may refer to his article on Paul the Apostle in Hastings' Dictionary of the Bible, volume 3; also to the article entitled Chronology of the New Testament in volume 1. Since the first edition of this work appeared, he has been led, by Ramsay's arguments, to adopt a.d. 49 instead of 51 as the date of the Jerusalem Council, but it still seems improbable to him that Paul's conversion took place so early as 33, the date adopted by Ramsay. Fixing the conversion at 36 and the Council in 49, we count the "three years" of Galatians 1:18 as part of the "fourteen" of Galatians 2:1, the apostle taking in both reckonings the time of his conversion as his starting point, since this was the birthday of his Christian life.

The Form and Style
of Paul's Writings

The teaching of the apostle Paul has come down to us in the shape of a bundle of his letters, thirteen in number, addressed some of them to individual friends and helpers in his work, but most of them to the Christian societies that he had founded. They are not treatises directed to the proof of theological doctrine, nor are they homilies devoted to the enforcement of specific practical duties: they are *letters* of a friend to his friends, of the absent missionary and pastor to his flock.[1] Their peculiar character and construction, and the mode in which the apostle's views are set forth in them, are determined by their epistolary form.

Personal and Incidental Writings

We must keep before our minds the fact that we are dealing with *personal documents*, writings which originate in the relationship of the writer and readers. The mutual acquaintance and affection of the two parties, their common interests and affairs, supply the basis on which

---

1. The epistle to the Romans is an exception to this rule and approaches in some degree the form of a systematic doctrinal treatise. But even with this church the apostle has many personal ties, on the strength of which, and in order to prepare for his coming, he addresses to it his great theological letter. The Colossian Christians he felt to be, through Epaphras, as his own children in the faith, though he had never set eyes upon them.

rest the communications that pass between them. The personal element is the primary and essential factor in all genuine Epistles.

It is from this personal standpoint that all questions, whether of theology or morals or church administration, that arise in Paul's letters are, in reality, approached. They come before us in the shape in which they actually emerged, as problems exercising the minds of Paul and his friends and converts, as, in fact, *the questions of the hour to them*. By means of the Epistles we can watch and trace these questions springing out of the constitution and surroundings of the young apostolic churches, and presenting themselves one after another for discussion and settlement. So these writings give to the subjects of which they treat the living interest and actuality that belong to the career of the great apostle, and to his labors in the care and shepherding of his strangely mingled flock.

With this personal origin is connected the fact that Paul's epistles are *incidental writings*. They were not composed, as letters between friends sometimes may be, according to a fixed plan and at regular intervals, but as occasion arose, to meet some passing necessity, to give expression to some feeling or wish that possessed the writer's mind at the time. He writes to Corinth, because the church there has written to him asking a number of urgent questions (1 Cor. 7:1; 8:1; 12:1), and because he has "been informed concerning you . . . by Chloe's *people* that there are quarrels among you" (1 Cor. 1:11); to the Colossians, since Epaphras, their minister, has come to Rome, telling him of the love borne to him by the churches of the Lycus valley which he has never seen, and describing the insidious error that endangered their faith (Col. 1:4–9; 4:12, 13); to Philippi, on the occasion of Epaphroditus arriving with a welcome contribution to his need from its affectionate people (Phil. 2:25, 30; 4:18). And yet through these disconnected and seemingly casual letters of Paul, thrown off on the spur of the occasion and under the most various circumstances—in the intervals of travel, in prison, or from his winter quarters—there runs one master purpose, one great system of truth, one ever-widening and deepening conception of human life and the things of God. The variety of circumstances, one might almost say, of *accidents*, to which the Epistles owe their origin, and the entire absence of plan and arrangement on the writer's part in their composition, make the unity and the continuous march of thought that we find in them the more impressive.

Style Attractive, but Difficult

The style of the Epistles, while due chiefly to the writer's temperament and training, is yet determined to a large extent by the conditions above described. It is said, "The style is the man," and this is eminently true of epistolary style. Hence, not unfrequently, the letters of a gifted writer are more attractive than his labored works, just because of the absence in them of literary effort and artifice, because they are written out of the freedom of the heart and are the frank and spontaneous expression of the man. Paul's epistles have this engaging quality, at once their difficulty and their charm. "The epistolary style of Paul," says M. Renan, "is the most personal that ever was. One might describe it as a rapid conversation, reported verbatim and without correction." There is nothing in literature more transparent, nothing that exhibits in a more vivid and moving way the personality of the writer.

Now Paul's is *not an easy style*. For he was not a man who took things easily. Life was for him a continual struggle, inwardly as well as outwardly. Underneath the activity of his missionary life or the calm of his prison days, there was going on within him an unceasing effort and striving to "lay hold of that for which also [he] was laid hold of by Christ Jesus" (Phil. 3:12). He is laboring to bring to birth thoughts of God too large for human speech, "the mystery which for ages has been hidden in God . . . to know the love of Christ which surpasses knowledge" (Eph. 3:9, 19) and search its unfathomed depths. This conflict becomes in his epistles a conflict between thought and speech, between the might of the spirit and the infirmity of the flesh. The wrestling and strain of the apostle's mind are manifest in the involved, contorted sentences of which many of his great passages consist. With broken outcries and halting yet impetuous utterance, he sweeps us breathless through his long periods, as he pursues far up the steep some lofty thought, while language threatens every moment to break down under the weight it is compelled to carry, until at last he reaches his magnificent climax and the tangled path through which he has forced his way lies clear beneath our feet. Great as were the resources of the apostle's dialect, yet they are insufficient, and he is continually coining new words or filling with a new content, which overflows them, the old phrases of the Greco-Jewish schools.

Paul was a pioneer in thought and religion. It was his work to open a pathway for the truth of Christ to the conscience and intellect of the Gentile world, to translate the "salvation" that was "from the Jews" for the understanding of mankind. It was a task of extreme difficulty, and has been achieved with wonderful success, but that difficulty has left its mark on the style of the apostle of the Gentiles, even as his lame thigh was a witness to wrestling Jacob's victory.

This subtle and eager thinker was, at the same time, a man of ardent feeling. Paul's passionate disposition was sanctified, but not destroyed, by divine grace. His fine sensibility of temperament gave to his address the peculiar delicacy and tact by which it is characterized, notwithstanding his frequent abruptness, and to that temperament equally belong his extraordinary fire, rapidity, and vehemence. Much of the obscurity and involvement of his language is caused by contending undercurrents of feeling in him, by the quick play of emotion in his singularly mobile nature. In the soul of the apostle Paul, logic and sentiment, passion and severe thought, were fused into a combination of unexampled pliancy, tenderness, and strength.

While his style has, therefore, its characteristic defects and was, not unnaturally, considered by Corinthian critics wanting in "superiority of speech or of wisdom" (1 Cor. 2:1), it was for all that one of the keenest instruments that a human mind has ever wielded. In the construction of his sentences and the connection of one phrase with another there is frequent uncertainty, arising from the very throng and pressure of his thoughts: the thoughts themselves, when you once discern them, are admirably clear and luminous. There is nothing hazy, nothing loose or nebulous, in Paul's theology. His leading terms, the great watchwords of his doctrine, are framed to last forever. They are as crystalline in definition as they are massive and deep in significance. His governing ideas are developed and applied with matchless logic, a logic, indeed, more rabbinical than philosophical in form, but that goes straight as an arrow to its mark, and that welds into its argument as it moves onward things highest and lowliest and seizes at each point the readiest expedient to clear its course and to build up the highway for the ransomed of the Lord.

Bold as are Paul's methods of reasoning, they are no less sure. His subtlety is the subtlety of truth itself. His obscurities are those of depth not of dimness or confusion, the obscurities of a mind profoundly sensible of the complexities of life and thought and sensitive to their varying hues, their crossing lights and shadows, of a man who, with all he knows, is conscious that he only "knows in part." If we must speak of *defects*, they are the defects of a teacher who is too full of the grandeur of the truth he utters, and too much absorbed in the divine work of his calling, to make words and style his care. "But even if I am unskilled in speech," he gently says, "yet I am not so in knowledge" (2 Cor. 11:6). In this, as in his other infirmities, well might the apostle glory.

Order and Contents of the Epistles

As to *the order of procedure* in Paul's epistles: they begin with the salutation of "Grace to you and peace," which appears to be of his own coining, "mercy" being tenderly inserted in the letters to Timothy. This salutation is variously qualified and expanded, in some instances serving to strike already the keynote of the epistle. A thanksgiving is next offered to God for the special Christian excellencies discerned in his correspondents, usually supplemented by an appropriate prayer on their behalf. It is after this act of devotion that the object of the letter comes into view, and where, as in Romans or Colossians, that object is theological, we may look for some fundamental statement of doctrine at this point. The doctrine asserted is then explained and vindicated at large, in such fashion as circumstances may require, and the doctrinal exposition is followed up by the moral and practical teaching of the epistle. Details of personal news, messages and greetings, with a final benediction, conclude the letter. Such is the order of the theological epistles: Romans, Galatians, Ephesians, Colossians, and 2 Thessalonians.

Where, however, the writer's main business is of a personal or practical nature, this plan cannot be observed: the statements, explanations, or directions to be given concerning the matters calling for the letter naturally occupying the foreground, while exhortations of a more general character come in afterwards, and theological passages occur here and there as occasion suggests, and wherever the handling of the matter in question happens to strike upon the underlying spiritual principles of the apostle's teaching. This is the case, for example, with the two epistles to the Corinthians. The rich theological truth they contain is developed, for the most part, incidentally and by the way.

We shall find, therefore, that the contents of the Epistles may be classified under the following heads, as *personal, theological, ethical, administrative,* and *devotional.* These various topics and constituent elements run into each other and are combined in numberless ways. We cannot at any point draw a strict line between them. But it is the proportion in which they are blended and the preponderance of the one constituent or the other which give to each epistle its distinctive complexion. *Romans* is, above all others, the theological epistle. *Second Corinthians* and *Philippians* are intensely personal. In *1 Corinthians* and *the Pastorals* the practical and administrative interests predominate, with a large infusion both of the ethical and doctrinal. In *1 Thessalonians* the personal and ethical, in *Colossians* and *Ephesians* the doctrinal and ethical are equally balanced, with a conspicuous development of the devotional vein in the last named. *Galatians* is the best example of the union of the personal, theological, and moral in Paul's writings, the theological asserting its supremacy over the other two.

The Language of the Apostle

Paul, as a native of Tarsus, knew Greek from his childhood, and the refinements of its grammar and idiom come to him instinctively. His irregularities of style are never ungrammatical; they are due to the conversational freedom of his letters, and to the vivacity and subtlety of the writer's temperament. But behind the Greek dress lives a Hebrew spirit. Saul's youth was spent "educated under Gamaliel" (Acts 22:3), and his mind formed by the rabbinical discipline (Gal. 1:14). The basis of his vocabulary lies in the Septuagint; outside of Scripture, Philo Judaeus and Josephus supply its best illustrations. But the apostle's language and manner are original in a high degree. His mind was fertile in expression, as it was creative in thought. Each group of the Epistles contains words and phrases special to itself. Paul has no hackneyed formula. The variety and freshness of his language even increased with time. His speech reflects the color of its surroundings and adapts itself to altered situations. See on this point further page 127.

In general it may be said that the groundwork of the New Testament language is not the literary Greek of the day, as that is found for instance in Plutarch or Dio Chrysostom, still less the classical Attic of 400 years earlier, but the vernacular Greek of the Levant in the first century before and after Christ.

To the Thessalonians

The two epistles to the Thessalonians form the *first group* of Paul's extant letters. They are probably the earliest writings of the New Testament. In respect of their general characteristics, we may style them *missionary letters, and* in view of the doctrine prominent in them, *epistles of the Second Advent.* They were written, as we have already shown, during the apostle's second missionary journey, when he planted his first European churches, and was in the full tide of evangelistic labor and triumph.

Date and Connection of the Two Letters

We date these epistles, with certainty, from the earlier part of Paul's eighteen months' residence at Corinth (Acts 18:11), that is, from the winter and spring of the year A.D. 50–51. In no other instance are the occasion and mutual relation of any of Paul's writings so easily made out as in this pair of letters. The second letter was sent shortly after the first, of which it is almost a continuation. It deals in explanation and further enforcement of the same leading topics (cf. 1 Thess. 1:10; 4:15–17 with 2 Thess. 2:1; 5:1–10, 23; 1 Thess. 4:11, 12; 5:14: "admonish the unruly" with 2 Thess. 3:6–15;). The situation and state of the church, as indicated in the two epistles, are much the same (cf. 1 Thess. 1:3, 6; 2:14; 3:2, 4–10; 4:1: NAS, 9, 10 with 2 Thess. 1:3–5; 3:4); certain evils to which the first letter called attention have been aggravated in the interval between the two. In vocabulary and

turn of expression, and in the mood of the writer's mind in the two
epistles, there is a close resemblance manifest to every attentive
reader, such as does not exist in the case of writings of the apostle separated by any considerable distance of time.

Now, the first epistle was dispatched not long after Paul's mission
to Thessalonica. A few months, at most, had elapsed since the establishment of the church. This the whole tenor of the letter shows.
The apostle dwells in the first two chapters on the coming of the missionaries to this city, on the reception of the gospel there, on the conversion of his readers to the new faith and the character and spirit of
their Christian life in its beginning. From this he draws the material
for his thanksgivings to God, and for his commendations and en-
couragements of his persecuted flock. No more recent event, no
later stage of experience, either on his part or on theirs, is so much
as mentioned. First Thessalonians 4:13–18 gives decisive evidence of
the fact that 1 Thessalonians was addressed to a church in the very
infancy of its Christian growth. The apostle "do[es] not want" his
brethren at Thessalonica "uninformed . . . about those who are
asleep" (more strictly, *are falling asleep*). Death had begun to visit this
brotherhood. The survivors were seized by a strange fear lest their departed friends, dying before the Lord's return, should have thereby lost
their place and their share in His approaching advent. This question
had evidently arisen among them *for the first time, and* it is never long,
alas! in any community, of size beyond the smallest, before death takes
his tribute from its ranks.

Paul gives an account of his proceedings since leaving Thessalonica. He departed most unwillingly, with the intention of returning soon to complete his work, which was left in an unfinished state
(1 Thess. 2:17; 3:10). He had conceived a very tender regard for this
society, and left it exposed to a furious storm of persecution (1 Thess.
2:8, 19, 20; 3:3, 4, 12). Since his departure an intolerable apprehension had possessed his mind on its account. Twice he attempted
to return, but in vain. At considerable sacrifice, he had sent Timothy
from Athens in his place (1 Thess. 3:1–5). Timothy has now returned,
joining the apostle at Corinth (Acts 18:5), and bringing tidings
that give him intense satisfaction and are as new life to him in his ar-
duous work at Corinth (1 Thess. 3:6–10). At once he sits down to
write, out of a deeply moved heart, this grateful, affectionate, and fa-

therly epistle. It is the letter of a father in Christ to his disciples and dear friends; of a missionary to a band of converts but newly gathered out of heathenism, to a church "in its earliest love," whose faith wears the freshness and eager enthusiasm of youth and morning hours, not without the defects of knowledge which riper experience and instruction will correct.

Paul's narrative and the references to his connection with Thessalonica, given in 1 Thessalonians 1—3, should be compared throughout with the full account of the mission to Macedonia and Achaia contained in Acts 17, 18. At no other point have we material for comparison between Acts and the Epistles so detailed and continuous as these documents afford. The story told by Luke agrees as fully as could be desired, in a manifestly independent way and in a number of coincidences lying below the surface, with the notices of place and circumstance given by the apostle, and this agreement tends strongly to verify the genuineness and historical accuracy of both the writings thus compared.

Occasion of the Epistles

The apostle wrote to these people, because he could not go to see them. This was due, indeed, to Jewish persecution and that "Satan thwarted us" (1 Thess. 2:18). At the same time, it marks a new juncture in Paul's career as apostle of the Gentiles. The churches founded upon his first tour lay comparatively near to Antioch, his original headquarters, and could all be visited from that center in the course of a few months. It was otherwise when his mission-field extended to Europe and included two continents. From this time it was impossible for him to superintend the churches he had founded without the aid of messengers and letters. He is obliged to *write*, and to have a staff of helpers whom he may send backwards and forwards between himself and distant Christian societies. To this growth and enlargement of the field of his labors we owe the apostolic letters. The circumstances that called forth these epistles are not far to seek:

The *persecution* that had driven Paul and his companions from Thessalonica (Acts 17:5–10) still continued in a violent and harassing form, severely testing the faith and resolution of the infant church (1 Thess. 1:6; 3:2–8; 2 Thess. 1:4–7). It originated with *the Jews* of the city, whose hostility pursued the missionaries to Berea, and Paul was experiencing, or expecting, similar treatment from his compatriots in Corinth at the very time of writing. Hence the stern denunciation which he delivers against them in 1 Thessalonians 2:14–16.

From the same quarter, doubtless, proceeded the *false insinuations against Paul and his colleagues*, to which he replies in 1 Thessalonians 2 and 3. Corrupt and selfish motives were imputed to them (1 Thess. 2:2–6), and his departure and continued absence from Thessalonica were put down to fear on his own account, or to indifference to the fate of his suffering followers. Slanders of this kind were the natural resort of Jewish cunning. The pains which the apostle takes to exculpate himself to his readers (1 Thess. 2:1–12), the earnestness and warmth of protestation with which he dwells upon his affection towards them and concern for their welfare (1 Thess. 2:7, 8; 2:17—3:11), are explained at once when we consider that their ears were incessantly plied with malicious suggestions against the absent missionaries of Christ, whom, after all, they had known but for a short time.

The apostles had spoken much at Thessalonica concerning *the return of the Lord Jesus from heaven and the future kingdom of God* (1 Thess. 1:10; 2:12, 19; 3:13; 4:14; 5:23, 24; 2 Thess. 1:5, 10; 2:1, 5, 14). What they said on the subject had impressed the Thessalonians very deeply, but their words had been exaggerated and misunderstood in various ways. Some feared that their dead, or dying, friends would be shut out of the approaching kingdom (1 Thess. 4:13–18); others were busy calculating "the times and the epochs" (1 Thess. 5:1). There were those who presumed, notwithstanding the admonitions of the first letter, to announce that "the day of the Lord has come," and who even claimed the apostle's authority for this declaration (2 Thess. 2:1, 2).

The agitation prevailing on this subject had assumed a morbid and dangerous character. In some cases it produced wild excitement (2 Thess. 2:2); in others, unreasonable sorrow and alarm (1 Thess. 4:13; 2 Thess. 2:2). Several members of the church took occasion to leave their employment, bringing the burden of their maintenance on the society and disregarding the remonstrance of its officers; the kindly and guarded reproof given to this party in the first epistle (1 Thess. 2:9; 4:10–12; 5:12–14) failed to effect their amendment, and

Paul is compelled to deal openly and sternly with the offenders in writing a second time (2 Thess. 3:6–15). These extravagances disposed the more sober-minded to contemn supernatural gifts (1 Thess. 5:19–22), and by the conflicts of temper and opinion thus excited the peace of the whole church was seriously impaired (1 Thess. 5:13, 14; 2 Thess. 3:15, 16).

Character and Affinities of the Epistles

In the main, the teaching of these epistles is simple and elementary. There is no theoretical error to be corrected, no great doctrine to be expounded. They belong to an early period in the development of Gentile Christianity, and to an early phase of the apostle's doctrine, antecedent to the great controversy respecting Justification and Salvation by Faith. It is singular that in all their eight chapters the death of Christ is only once mentioned (1 Thess. 5:8–11), the cross not even once, and there is some plausibility in what Jowett said in his commentary, that the gospel Paul preached to the Thessalonians was "not the gospel of the cross of Christ, but of the coming of Christ." In reality, it was both. The second could have no comfort or joy attending it, would, in fact, be no *gospel*, no "glad tidings," without the first. This is shown plainly enough by Paul's words in the passage just referred to. The whole Pauline theology of the cross is involved in what is there said of "obtaining salvation through our Lord Jesus Christ" (1 Thess. 5:9). This teaching was so readily received and well understood at Thessalonica, that there was no need to expound or enforce it by letter. The atonement of Christ is the presupposition of all that is written in these two epistles, and they are no less evangelical, because it is but once expressly mentioned.

In their simple and practical character, in the comparative absence of censure and of controversy, and in the warmth of reciprocal affection between the apostle and his readers which the epistles to the Thessalonians manifest, they resemble the delightful letter written ten years later to the Philippians, their nearest neighbors. These characteristics justify us in styling the three in common *Macedonian epistles*.

By their general tone and subject-matter these writings associate themselves with Paul's *missionary preaching*, of which we have specimens in Acts 14 and 17, rather than with the great dogmatic and polemical epistles of the second group. First Thessalonians 1:9, with its emphatic contrast between "idols" and "a living and true God," reminds us forcibly of the apostle's addresses to the men of Lystra and of Athens. Throughout this letter the greatest emphasis is laid on the fact that the gospel is God's message and brings believers into new and exalted relations to God, to His kingdom and glory. Along with the nature of God, *the coming of Christ to judge the world* was the theme of Paul's sermon at the Areopagus, and this prospect is more conspicuous in the Thessalonian than in any other of Paul's epistles. The doctrine of the Last Judgment was a powerful instrument of the apostle's evangelistic work. That such a judgment would certainly take place and was committed to the hands of Jesus Christ, while sufficiently alarming to Felix and his like, was "good news" for every honest and good heart in a world where wickedness had so long and insolently triumphed, and its declaration, Paul emphatically says, is "according to my gospel" (Rom. 2:16). We have designated these writings *missionary letters*, since they belong to a time when the writer's preoccupations were of a missionary character, and because they were addressed to a young missionary church still subject to the persecutions and trials attending its birth.

The doctrine on which these two letters lay their stress and emphasis is that of the *parousia,* or Second Advent of Christ. They compel us to remember, what in these later times we are apt to forget, that the coming of the Lord Jesus is an essential and glorious part of the Christian faith and of God's message to mankind. Though so much is said upon the subject, it is discussed, after all, in a somewhat incidental fashion, by way of explanation and caution, not of full dogmatic statement, and its treatment presents points of very great difficulty. This is especially the case in the apostle's prediction of *the coming of Antichrist* (2 Thess. 2:1–12), which the original readers, remembering his previous oral teaching, understood with a clearness that is unattainable by ourselves. What he now writes is but a supplement to what he had previously said, and was to be interpreted in the light of his spoken words (2 Thess. 2:5, 6). This subject in later epistles retires into the background so that we depend largely on these documents for our knowledge of Paul's eschatological views, his doctrine of the Last Things. In fact, 1 Thessalonians 4:13–18 and 2 Thessalonians 2:1–12, together with 1 Corinthians 15:35–58, form *the Pauline apocalypse*. They occupy in our apostle's writings a position corresponding to that of the book of Revelation in those of John, and of the visions of Daniel in the Old Testament.

ANALYSIS: On a general view of the two epistles, we find that they contain: (1) *encouragement* to the readers under persecution (1 Thess. 1–3; 2 Thess. 1), blended with thanksgiving to God on their account, in which the apostle dwells on the signal nature of their conversion, on the courage and fidelity they had already shown, and the glory and certainty of their heavenly reward; (2) *self-defense* on the writer's part (1 Thess. 2, 3), who without referring directly to the reproaches made against him, yet warmly vindicates his conduct and gives strong proof of his affection towards the Thessalonians; (3) *explanation* on various points touching the Second Advent (1 Thess. 4:13—5:11; 2 Thess. 2:1–12); (4) *warnings* directed against idleness and disorder (1 Thess. 4:11, 12; 5:12–15; 2 Thess. 3:6–16), and against unchastity, the special vice of Greek cities (1 Thess. 4:1–8); (5) *prayers and exhortations* intermingled with these warnings, bearing chiefly on consecration to God, and on peace and brotherhood within the church (1 Thess. 3:11–13; 4:9, 10; 5:12–25; 2 Thess. 3:16).

Taking the epistles separately, and in their own order, we may divide them into the following sections:

1 THESSALONIANS   Address and Salutation, 1 Thessalonians 1:1.

§ 1. The Thanksgiving, and reasons for it, 1 Thessalonians 1:2–10.

§ 2. The apostle's conduct at Thessalonica, 1 Thessalonians 2:1–12.

§ 3. (Parenthetical) Jewish persecutors of the church, 1 Thessalonians 2:13–16.

§ 4. Paul's present relations to the Thessalonians, 1 Thessalonians 2:17—3:13.

§ 5. A lesson in Christian morals, 1 Thessalonians 4:1–12:
(a) On Chastity, 1 Thessalonians 4:1–8; (b) on Brotherly Love, 1 Thessalonians 4:9, 10; (c) on Quiet Diligence, 1 Thessalonians 9:11, 12.

§ 6. The Coming of the Lord Jesus, 1 Thessalonians 4:13—5:11:
(a) Concerning them that fall asleep, 1 Thessalonians 4:13–18; (b) concerning the day of the Lord, 1 Thessalonians 5:1–11.

§ 7. Rules for the Sanctified Life, 1 Thessalonians 5:12–24.

Conclusion, containing a solemn request "to have the letter read to all the brethren," 1 Thessalonians 5:25–28.

2 THESSALONIANS

§ 1. Salutation, and Thanksgiving, 2 Thessalonians1:1–4.
§ 2. The approaching Retribution, 2 Thessalonians 1:5–12.
§ 3. The Revelation of the Lawless One, 2 Thessalonians 2:1–12.
§ 4. Words of Comfort and Prayer, 2 Thessalonians 2:13—3:5.
§ 5. Discipline for the Disorderly, 2 Thessalonians 3:6–15.
Conclusion, calling attention to the writer's signature, 2 Thessalonians
    3:16–18.

We append brief explanations, by way of paraphrase, of the four
most difficult paragraphs of the epistles:[3]
First Thessalonians 4:1–8: "Before we close this letter, we have
some requests to make, which we urge upon you in the name of the
Lord Jesus: in general, that you follow the rules of life we gave you.
You *are* doing this, we know, but there is room for progress. In particular, be free from all taint of unchastity. Be masters of your bodily
passions. In this lies a great part of your sanctification. Lust, with its
dishonor, is the mark of Gentile godlessness. This sin brings wrong and
injury on others, while it degrades the man himself. The Lord is the
avenger of every offense against social purity. By such offense you set
Him at defiance, and outrage His Holy Spirit given to you."
First Thessalonians 4:13–18: "Death has been busy among you,
and your sorrow is deepened by a needless fear lest your sleeping
friends should have lost their part in the hope of Christ's return and
their place in His heavenly kingdom. Be comforted! His resurrection
from the dead is a pledge of theirs. God will restore them at His return. *They* will have indeed the first and foremost share in His glorious advent. At His trumpet's call they will rise from their sleep; we
who live on the earth will rejoin them, and together, in one body, we
shall ascend to meet our returning Lord. With Him we and they shall
then dwell forever!"
First Thessalonians 5:23, 24: "Above all, may God Himself,
Source and Giver of peace, accomplish your full sanctification! In the

---

3. These renderings are freely made and are an attempt to put the apostle's
thoughts, in a form as clear as possible, into our own words. Only when we can do
this with some correctness, have we thoroughly digested them and made them ours.

integrity of a consecrated spirit, soul, and body, may you be preserved and found without blame at Christ's coming. God has called you for this end. He is faithful: it shall be done."

Second Thessalonians 2:1–12: Paul has one principal and urgent purpose in writing now. It touches "the coming of our Lord Jesus Christ," in regard to which he desires to remove a dangerous and disturbing impression existing in Thessalonica, to the effect that "the day of the Lord [w]as come!" How this rumor originated, it was hard to say, whether through supposed prophetic intimation, or the ordinary teaching of the church, or from some misunderstanding or abuse of the apostle's written words, but its disastrous effect is manifest, and its *falsity*.

"I gave a token," the apostle writes, "of that which must precede the final coming of Christ: there will be first *the apostasy*, and *the revelation of the Man of Lawlessness*, the great enemy of God. He will attempt to annihilate religion, and will seat himself in God's temple as the sole object of human worship. The spirit of atheistic lawlessness, to be incarnated in him, is already actively at work, but for the present *under restraint*, as I pointed out to you. One day, however, the restraint will be withdrawn, and then the Lawless One will stand revealed! whom the Lord Jesus by His breath will consume and destroy by the splendor of His coming! Satan will instigate the great Opposer, and attest his coming by miracles suited to deceive those whose hearts are inclined to falsehood. Their deception will be the fit punishment for their rejection of the truth of God, and their love of lies and wickedness."

ADDITIONAL NOTE: Except in 2 Thessalonians 2:1–12; 3:6–15, 2 Thessalonians contains few expressions or ideas not already found in 1 Thessalonians. The repetition is such as has no parallel in Paul, until we come to the Pastoral Epistle, but its want of originality is no sufficient ground for doubting the authenticity of 2 Thessalonians. The two letters both purport to come from *three* writers, and possibly Silas, or Timothy, had a considerable share in the composition of the Second.

The Four
Evangelical Epistles

The Thessalonian letters contain very little that bears directly on what we are accustomed to call *the doctrines of salvation*. With the exception of 1 Thessalonians 5:8–10, there is no statement whatever made in those epistles on the subject of the atonement of Christ and the efficacy of faith in His blood. In the second group of Paul's writings, to which we now pass, the case is entirely altered. Here the cross meets us at every turn, "before whose eyes Jesus Christ was publicly portrayed as crucified" (Gal. 3:1). As these are beyond question the greatest of the apostle's letters, so beyond question the cross of Jesus Christ is the greatest and most conspicuous object in them.

It was the defense of "the word of the cross" that called forth all his powers and roused them to their full exercise. Through that defense, carried on in the Corinthian, Galatian, and Roman letters, we find our way to the heart of the man himself and to the heart of his theology. Here we learn the secret of the spell by which he moved the world of his own times, and moves it still with so potent a sway. Paul's other letters are great and inspired compositions, but half their greatness comes from their association with these. "I determined not to know anything among you, save Jesus Christ, and Him crucified" (1 Cor. 2:2). Such is the mood in which he now takes up his pen. These words, all but prefixed to the first of the epistles of the third missionary journey, might serve as motto to the group. They are written from the standpoint of Calvary. Christ's atonement forms their central and dominant theme, as His Second Advent that of the

epistles to the Thessalonians. For this reason we entitle them col-
lectively *the evangelical epistles*, and we shall discuss in this chapter
their common features and surroundings.

During the four or five years that had elapsed since the writing of
1 and 2 Thessalonians many things had happened. Most of this interval the apostle had spent at Ephesus, preaching there with a success exceeding anything he had known before so that the foundations
were laid of a large and vigorous church in Ephesus, and Christianity spread through the neighboring towns, reaching, as we afterwards find, even without Paul's presence, the city of Colossae on the
verge of the province of Asia (Acts 19:10–20; Col. 2:1). Meanwhile, the apostle was watching anxiously the course of affairs in the
churches of Galatia to the east, and of Corinth to the west beyond
the Aegean. Galatia he had revisited on his recent journey across the
peninsula from Antioch (Acts 18:22, 23; 19:1), and he discerned already symptoms that alarmed him, of a tendency towards Jewish rit-
ualism, alien from the spirit of the gospel (Gal. 1:9). Troubles of
another kind had arisen at Corinth, in reference to which the apostle had written a letter, brief apparently and confined to a single topic,
previously to our first extant epistle (1 Cor. 5:9). We gather also from
1 and 2 Corinthians that Paul paid a short visit to Corinth during the
last year of his residence in Ephesus (A.D. 55), "a year ago," reckoning from the time of his journey through Macedonia (2 Cor. 9:2),
when he saw distressing signs of disorder and impurity in the church
there and severely threatened the offenders, promising to return
before long "with a rod" if the cause of offense were not removed (see
1 Cor. 4:18–21; 2 Cor. 2:1; 12:14, 20—13:2).

The Judaizing movement, so pronounced in Galatia, had its rep-
resentatives in Corinth also among those who proclaimed, "I [am] of
Cephas" (1 Cor. 1:12). This church contained many conflicting elements, amidst which the first epistle reveals two opposite currents,
the one running in the direction of license, the other of legalism. In
the interval between Paul's writing 1 and 2 Corinthians, the party of
license was repressed, but the Judaistic party had meanwhile been
strengthened and its hostility to the apostle aggravated and em-
boldened by the introduction of a foreign influence, whose source and
whose working it will be necessary for us to trace.

The Conflict with Peter

Previous to all this, an event occurred which had, as we believe, a very close connection with the troubles in Galatia and Corinth, namely, *the collision of Paul with Peter at Antioch* (Gal. 2:11–21). This was a momentous epoch in apostolic history. The whole future of Christianity was involved in it. The fact that the contention broke out at Antioch, the center and mother city of the Gentile churches, where Barnabas and Paul, their two great founders, had for five years labored side by side, and that the entire body of the liberal Jewish Christians there, and "even Barnabas," Paul's earlier leader and almost his father in the faith, were "carried away" by the Judaistic agitation, and, above all, that "Cephas" lent his name to it, the apostle of Pentecost, who was far and away the most revered and influential man in the whole church, all this made the occasion one of extreme gravity and peril. Single as he stood, Paul resisted the entire force and weight of Jewish opinion. His remonstrance convicted Peter of "hypocrisy" and recalled him to his own better principles. But the error of the Jewish apostle, so openly committed and so well calculated to encourage the legalistic party, could not fail to have disastrous consequences.

The public reproof of Cephas, on whom the Judaists had fixed their hopes, drove them to desperate measures; indeed, this defeat rankled for a hundred years in the breasts of Jewish-Christian heretics, as their writings in the second century, the (so-called) Clementine Homilies and Recognitions, curiously show. They proceeded now to carry the war into the enemy's country. They made their way to the Pauline churches, where doubtless they found sympathizers among their countrymen, and they brought into play all the arts they could command to undermine the authority of the Gentile apostle, to poison the minds of his converts, and to graft the principles of their own Judaism upon the faith that Gentile believers had received from his lips. Added to all his other dangers and trials, the apostle now had "dangers among *false brethren*" (2 Cor. 11:26).

Emissaries of the legalistic party were following on Paul's track, setting out from Jerusalem and claiming, like those "certain men from James" (Gal. 2:12) who caused the mischief at Antioch, to be commissioned from the mother church. From this source they brought with them "letters of commendation," but they were "false apostles, deceitful workers," preachers of "a different gospel," teaching the Gentiles to be circumcised and to seek salvation by Jewish ritual and works of Law and making the cross of Christ void (2 Cor. 3:1; 11:13; Gal. 1:7; 5:2, 11; 6:13). We shall be able to trace their action more distinctly in examining the Galatian and Second Corinthian letters, but it is necessary to recognize here at the outset the existence and activity of the anti-Pauline, Judaistic party, if we are to understand the position in which Paul found himself at the time of writing these four epistles, and the condition of things to which they were addressed. It is only when we read in his letters between the lines the arguments and innuendoes of his opponents, that we gather the full force of his reasoning, his protestations and appeals. These are, in fact, the epistles of *the Judaistic controversy*, written in defense and vindication of the doctrine of the cross. They guide the church along the way of salvation by faith, and guard her from that other way of salvation by works of Law to which the feet of her children are ever and again in peril of being drawn aside.

This was the great controversy of Paul's life. It befell, fortunately, when he was in the vigor and maturity of his powers, and it stirred the very depths of his soul. He alone discerned the significance of the crisis. He understood thoroughly the sort of men he had to deal with, and the nature of their principles and methods, for he had been educated in their own school. His training and experience had fitted him precisely for the conflict in which he was engaged, as the champion of the cross and of Gentile liberties. The Spirit of God came mightily upon him, and he encountered the false apostles in the field of his Gentile mission with the same prompt courage and irresistible force with which he had already reproved the vacillation of his brother apostle at Antioch.

The manner in which the collision between the two apostles is described in the epistle to the Galatians shows that this occurrence had a very direct bearing on the controversy carried on in the Pauline churches. We have assumed that the contention occurred at the time of Paul's winter sojourn in Antioch (A.D. 52–53), immediately before he set out on his third missionary journey, during the course of which the Judaistic agitation shook the Achaian and Galatian churches. The attempt made by "certain men from James" to forbid Jewish Christians eating with the Gentiles, when looked at in the light of subsequent events, appears to have been the opening of a new campaign, the first step in carrying out a systematic plan for Judaizing Gentile Christianity. A mission was set on foot by the legalists of Jerusalem, men who were in reality unconverted, or half-converted, Pharisees, by which it was designed to bring the Pauline churches under the yoke of the Mosaic covenant and incorporate them with Israel after the flesh. At the council of Jerusalem, in the year 49 (Acts 15; Gal. 2:1–10), the legalists sustained a crushing defeat, and they can scarcely have dared to make this bold and public attack on the liberal Christianity of Antioch until some considerable time had elapsed. Still less likely is it that Peter, and "even Barnabas," on the very morrow of that decisive vindication of Gentile liberties in which they had taken so conspicuous and generous a part, were "carried away" by influences proceeding from the Judaistic camp. Moreover, Luke in Acts 15:30–41 gives us an extended account of what took place at Antioch after the council, without the least intimation that Peter at this time visited the Syrian capital. But on the occasion of Paul's next sojourn at Antioch, when he completed his second missionary tour, the bare fact is related of his arrival and his continuance there for some length of time (Acts 18:22, 23) so that nothing stands in the way of our supposing the visit of Peter to Antioch, intimated in Galatians 2, to have taken place at this particular time, in the interval between the second and third missionary journeys.

Finally, the two Thessalonian epistles, already examined, give no hint of any Judaistic controversy within the church between the years 49 and 52, antecedent to the date we have arrived at for the renewed outbreak of hostilities at Antioch. It is against "the" unbelieving and persecuting "Jews" outside the church, not against Judaizing "false brethren" within its pale, that Paul's indignation is expressed in 1 Thessalonians 2:14–16. In the first group of letters, the apostle's thoughts run in a direction very different from that given to them by the collision with Cephas at Antioch: they have not yet assumed the course which we find them pursuing with vehemence and concentrated energy in the epistles that lie before us.

> Evidently the apostle had quitted Jerusalem [after the council of A.D. 49] and undertaken his second missionary journey full of satisfaction at

the victory he had gained, and free from anxiety for the future. The decisive moment of the crisis, therefore, necessarily falls between the Thessalonian and Galatian epistles. What had happened in the meantime?
The violent discussion with Peter at Antioch (Gal. 2:11–21), and all that
this incident reveals to us, the arrival of the emissaries from James in
the Gentile Christian circle, the counter-mission organized by the Judaizers to rectify the work of Paul. A new situation suddenly presents
itself to the apostle on his return from his second missionary journey.
He is compelled to throw himself into the struggle.[1]

It is to the crisis brought about by the Jewish legalists and the
enormous peril which it involved, a peril revealed with startling effect by the "hypocrisy" of Peter and Barnabas, that we owe the existence of this group of epistles and everything distinctive in their
character. They were called forth by a great emergency. They are a
monument of the emancipation of Christianity from Judaism. They
are the charter of the rights of faith, the witness to the divine sonship
of believers and the universal heritage of mankind in Jesus Christ.
They are the full manifesto and expression of the mind of the apostle of the Gentiles, and of the mind of Christ towards the world declared through him.

Paul's Apostleship Disputed

With the doctrinal question at issue in these epistles, a personal
question was deeply involved, that of *Paul's apostolic standing*. His Jewish antagonists attacked his policy through himself. His authority as
a Christian teacher, his relations with the primitive church and its
chiefs, Cephas in particular, his conduct and management in the
church, even his infirmities and peculiarities of manner, were keenly
criticized. Every weapon was used against him that spiteful Jewish in-

---

1. *Sabatier:* "The Apostle Paul: a Sketch of the Development of his Doctrine"
(Hodder & Stoughton). The delightful work of A. Sabatier, ably translated from
the French, gives a graphic picture of the events and movements connected with
this momentous crisis. The writer takes this opportunity of acknowledging his great
indebtedness to Sabatier's most lucid (though theologically defective) exposition
of Paul's teaching. On the subject of the Judaistic agitation, he may also refer to the
Expositor's Bible (Gal.), chapters 6—10, where it is fully discussed.

genuity could suggest. Hence 2 Corinthians and Galatians contain an extended personal defense, a defense conducted, however, differently in the two letters, as the attack in these distant quarters had assumed a different form. The Judaistic impeachment, combined with the disorders of the church of Corinth, compelled Paul to the unqualified assertion of his apostolic office and powers.

The three "pillars" at Jerusalem, he tells us, had acknowledged him as their equal at the meeting of the year 49; they recognized his "apostleship . . . to the Gentiles" as similar and parallel to that conferred on Peter in regard to the Jews (Gal. 2:7–10). Yet in his subsequent letters to the Thessalonians we hear nothing of all this. "Gentle among" this affectionate people, he had no need to assert his prerogative, and in writing to them he raises himself in nowise above Silas and Timothy, who possessed in common with him the humbler apostleship that belongs to all Christian missionaries (1 Thess. 2:6). But there is need now for something more than gentleness. Throwing aside all reserve, the great apostle reveals his consciousness of the awful powers committed to him. He rises to the height of his office; he makes good his claim to be "an apostle (not *sent* from men, nor through the agency of man, but through Jesus Christ, and God the Father who raised Him from the dead)" (Gal. 1:1). Yet, in this height of Paul's self-exaltation, his deep personal humility is all the more apparent.

Practical Topics of these Epistles

Along with the doctrinal and personal topics, which possess such absorbing interest in these letters, we find a number of *practical questions* arising in the young Gentile Christian communities, that now begin to press upon the apostle's attention. At Corinth the leaven of the new faith had seized upon keen and active minds and brought within its influence the most diverse elements, and here quite a number of difficulties, ethical, social, and ecclesiastical—partly internal, partly arising from the contact of Christianity with Pagan and Jewish society, and some of them of the most delicate nature—cropped up all at once. And the apostle shows himself master of them all. Nowhere does his inspired sagacity, his moral insight and practical sense, shine with more luminous effect than in 1 Corinthians. Well does he vindicate his own saying, "But he who is spiritual appraises all things" (1 Cor.

2:15). Through this epistle we view as in a mirror the inner life and proceedings of an early Christian society; we see what the first Gentile converts were like, out of what strange material the church was created, and what discordant and intractable natures the Spirit of Christ had undertaken to control and assimilate. In this epistle also we detect the first traces of the philosophical and rationalistic ferment which gave rise to the Gnostic heresies of the following age. This influence is combated in its further development by the epistles of the third group, especially Colossians.

Genuineness of these Epistles

The letters of this group are the only New Testament writings whose authenticity is unquestioned by modern criticism. Before these writings, skepticism itself makes a respectful pause: so vivid and intense is the reality that pervades them; with so powerful an effect has the apostle stamped upon them his personality and the impress of his times. Whatever else may be doubted or denied, no one can reasonably doubt that there was such a man as Paul the apostle of Christ Jesus, and that he wrote these four epistles, within thirty years of his Master's death, to Christian societies then existing in Asia Minor, Corinth, and Rome: all but the last, of his own foundation. Now this is a historical fact of immense importance. For these four letters contain all the vital doctrines of the gospel; they presuppose, directly or indirectly, the essential facts touching the life and teaching, the death and resurrection of the Lord Jesus. Without a Christ such as we find in the four Gospels, the Paul of these four epistles is unintelligible. God "was pleased," the apostle says, "to reveal His Son in me"—the Son of God and Son of man who stands before us in the pages of Luke and John, and no other explanation of Paul's history—of his conversion, of his character, doctrine and achievements—has been given that is even tolerably plausible. If every other witness were destroyed or discredited, still these documents remain, an irrefutable proof of the truth and saving efficacy of "the gospel of God . . . concerning His Son, who was born of a descendant of David according to the flesh, who was declared the Son of God with power by the resurrection from the dead, according to the Spirit of holiness" (Rom. 1:1–4). The Paul of Romans, Corinthians, and Galatians, strict logic, and historical criticism compel us to accept the Jesus of the Evangelists. Such an effect as these letters set before us, demands an adequate cause. The only cause that can conceivably account for what Paul was, for what he has done and written, is "Jesus Christ is the same yesterday and today, yes and forever" (Heb. 13:8). He alone is the author of such faith, and He will be its finisher.

On the other side, we may argue from the admitted genuineness of these documents to the authorship of the rest of the Pauline epistles. Indeed, they supply us with a means of testing, more or less completely, the date and character of the New Testament writings generally. So successfully has this line of demonstration been prosecuted that, while fifty years ago the rationalistic school dominant in Germany allowed but four epistles to be the genuine products of Paul's pen, there are now only four remaining, out of the thirteen bearing his name (namely, Eph. and the three Pastorals), which the present leaders of that party unite in rejecting, and the three Synoptic Gospels, at that time so confidently referred to the second century, are today very generally admitted to have appeared before the end of the first.

It is difficult to exaggerate the importance which belongs to these four epistles in the defense and confirmation of the gospel, alike in face of sacerdotal and Romish perversions and of rationalistic denials of its truth. They furnish us with an impregnable fortress of our faith, planted in the midst of the New Testament, and they supply a fixed starting point and indubitable test for the examination of all questions touching the origin and nature of Christianity, and the history of the apostolic age.

Recent Criticism of the Epistles

The statement made on page 40, to the effect that the authenticity of the four Evangelical epistles is uncontested, requires at this date (1907) some qualification. There is now a group of scholars, chiefly Dutch critics and ably represented by Van Manen (art. Paul) in the new Encyclopedia Biblica, who maintain that no genuine letter of the original Paul is extant, and that even "Galatians" contains only fragments from his own hand. But their contention is of little account; it is viewed as paradoxical by the body even of "advanced" critics, and is in effect a reductio ad absurdum of the Tendency theory of F. C. Baur which was prevalent in Germany forty or fifty years ago.

The First to the Corinthians

The first to the Corinthians was, in all probability, the earliest of the four major epistles. It has been generally supposed that the letter to the Galatians came first in order of time. We shall see reason for placing it rather between 2 Corinthians and Romans, and its connection with the last-named is so close and intimate in order of thought, that even if the earlier date were established, it would still be desirable for interpretation to put these two writings side by side. We shall, therefore, first discuss the two Corinthian epistles, then in turn Galatians and Romans.

Date and Occasion of 1 Corinthians

The apostle's sojourn at Ephesus is drawing to a close. Easter is approaching (A.D. 56), and he expects to stay in the Asian capital until Pentecost, where "a wide door for effective service" is opened to him (1 Cor. 5:8; 16:8, 9). After Pentecost he proposes traveling to Macedonia and devoting the summer to that province, then coming on to Corinth and spending the ensuing winter there (1 Cor. 16:1–9), after that setting out to Jerusalem. Such is his program for the year. He had previously intended to come direct to Corinth from Ephesus and pay the Corinthian church a flying visit before commencing his summer work in Macedonia (2 Cor. 1:15, 16). This purpose he has abandoned, for reasons that will afterwards appear (2 Cor. 1:23; 12:20, 21).

43

Meanwhile, he has sent Timothy on the way to Corinth, by Macedonia, along with a certain Erastus (Acts 19:22; 1 Cor. 4:17). He supposes that Timothy will arrive shortly after the letter, and will be able to supplement its contents. But it was possible he might be hindered or delayed—Paul writes, "if Timothy comes" (1 Cor. 16:10), and so indeed it turned out. For in the second epistle, which Paul writes from Macedonia with Timothy by his side (2 Cor. 1:1), not a word is said of Timothy's mission to Corinth or of any news brought by him to the apostle (contrast with this 1 Thess. 3:6–8); Paul's mind is full of *Titus'* coming, and of what Titus has told him of the state of affairs at Corinth (2 Cor. 2:13; 7:5–16). Clearly it was Titus, and not Timothy, who actually went to Corinth. Finding, after he had written this letter, that Timothy would be unable to reach Corinth in time, or perhaps fearing that Timothy's gentle nature would prove unequal to encounter the turbulent Corinthians (see 1 Cor. 16:10, 11), the apostle dispatched Titus instead, to "remind" them "of [his] ways which are in Christ" (1 Cor. 4:17), to report to him on the condition of the church and the effect of the epistle just sent, and at the same time to expedite the collection for Jerusalem already commenced in Achaia (2 Cor. 9:2),which Paul wishes to see completed in preparation for his visit to the Holy City (1 Cor. 16:1–6).

This contribution in aid of "the poor among the saints" at Jerusalem is mentioned or alluded to in all the letters of this period (Rom. 15:25–29; cf. Acts 24:17, and, probably, Gal. 2:10, 6:7–10). We are told in 2 Corinthians 8:6 that Titus took a special interest in this work of charity, arising perhaps from the fact that he had been with Paul at Jerusalem some years before (Gal. 2:1), and therefore was acquainted with the necessities of the Christian poor in that city.

Previous to the dispatch of our first extant epistle, there had been a good deal of communication between Paul and Corinth, the course of which we cannot, however, make out with certainty. From 2 Corinthians 12:14; 13:1, 2 ("the *third* time I am ready to come to you"), we infer that *he had himself visited the Corinthian church* not very long ago, when he was grieved and humbled exceedingly by the moral laxity, the strife, disorder, and insolence that he witnessed among its members (2 Cor. 12:20, 21). It is possible that we have a hint of the time of this visit in 2 Corinthians 9:2, where the words "since last year," if referring to the apostle's presence in "Achaia," indicate the summer or autumn of 55 as the date of his excursion from Ephesus.

This trip to Corinth made but a brief interruption in his labors in Asia, and is therefore unrecorded in Acts, but it left a deep and saddening impression on the apostle's mind. He took no judicial action against the offenders at the time, contenting himself with hearing "the words of those who are arrogant" (for to this occasion we think he alludes in 1 Cor. 4:19), and warning them of the punishment that would ensue if on his return in the next spring he found them unrepentant (2 Cor. 13:2). This forbearance some of his opponents put down to weakness on his part, an impression that he fears may be aggravated by the present delay in his coming, and which in both epistles he earnestly strives to remove (1 Cor. 4:18–21; 2 Cor. 1:17—2:1), promising his defiers, who asked for "proof of the Christ who speaks in [him]" (2 Cor. 13:2, 3), that their wish would shortly be gratified. The antecedent visit whose occurrence we learn from the second epistle, helps to explain the situation in which Paul finds himself toward the Corinthians in writing the first, and the full knowledge of their condition which the letter manifests.

Not only had Paul been in Corinth a few months before this time, he had also *written* to the church there *a letter*, probably in consequence of his visit, and to this letter he refers in 1 Corinthians 5:9, "I wrote you in my letter not to associate with immoral people." The single reference made to it suggests that this was a brief peremptory note, directing the church to purge itself from fellowship with unchaste men. Its purport, however, was misunderstood, so that Paul has to explain and qualify it in 1 Corinthians 5:9–13. It is conjectured that we have, after all, a paragraph of the earlier lost letter in 2 Corinthians 6:14—7:1, that has somehow slipped into this place. This passage very much interrupts the connection of thought where we find it in 2 Corinthians, and it is well suited to the purpose of the letter alluded to in 1 Corinthians 5. The Corinthians received this authoritative note from Paul, but had not as yet acted upon it. The doubt raised as to its meaning supplied an excuse for delay. In explaining this by letter to the apostle, they addressed to him at the same time a number of inquiries, with which he deals consecutively in 1 Corinthians 7—12.

Three esteemed members of the Corinthian church, Stephanas, Fortunatus, and Achaicus, had also arrived at Ephesus. They came seemingly as a deputation, bringing with them the above letter, and wishful to reassure the anxious apostle as to the feeling of the Corinthians towards him (1 Cor. 16:17, 18). Unfortunately, about the same time, he heard from another source, "by Chloe's people" (1 Cor. 1:11), tidings which revived his worst fears. The strifes he had witnessed with so much sorrow had broken out still more violently; indeed, they threatened to bring about the speedy disruption of the church. Amid the general rivalry and confusion, four separate factions were distinguished. There were the *Judaists*, destined to play an important part in the later development of affairs, who said, "I [am] of Cephas" (1 Cor. 1:12). The *Apollos* party, admirers of the eloquent Alexandrine preacher, who had made a great impression at Corinth since Paul's first mission there, but who was now at Ephesus with the apostle (Acts 19:1; 1 Cor. 16:12) and unwilling at present to return: these boasted themselves men of culture and philosophic breadth; they missed in the apostle's discourse the "superiority of speech or of wisdom" with which Apollos had gratified them (1 Cor. 2:1; 2 Cor. 11:6). Nor did *Paul* lack vigorous asserters of his superiority, men devoted to evangelic faith and freedom, whose championship, however, was maintained with a party spirit highly distasteful to him. Even the name of Christ was dragged into these wretched competitions. There was a *Christian* party as jealous and disputatious as the rest, who set themselves above their brethren in claiming to be the true followers of Jesus, disparaging all other names and all earthly authority in the pride of saying, "I [am] of Christ" (1 Cor. 1:12).

In the feuds and embroilment of these factions the disorders of the Corinthian church came to a head, and to this contention Paul directs his first expostulations. For the present, the Apollonian party is that which gave him most concern, and to them 1 Corinthians 1—4 are mainly addressed (observe that *Apollos'* name occurs six times in these chs.). To their philosophical bias was due the disbelief in a bodily resurrection, which the apostle combats in 1 Corinthians 15, and the magnifying of "knowledge" and intellectual gifts, which he corrects by his exaltation of "love" in 1 Corinthians 8:1–8, 13. From members of this party also proceeded the disparagement of Paul himself, the contempt of his power and ingratitude for his services against which he asserts himself with pathetic dignity in the early pages of the letter.

Among the cases of immorality that had occurred in this church (2 Cor. 12:21), there was one of an especially shameful nature, respecting which Paul has now received information that leaves no room for doubt as to the facts (1 Cor. 5:1). The church appeared to be little sensible of the disgrace thus brought upon it (1 Cor. 5:2). Instead of taking immediate action according to the tenor of Paul's instructions, it had temporized, writing to him in self-complacent terms and requesting further explanation of his meaning. Manifestly, it was in no haste to remove the vicious leaven. He demands indignantly a prompt and summary judgment of the case, so that before the approaching Passover the church may be purged of the profligate's defiling presence (1 Cor. 5:3–13).

This case of discipline was a crucial matter. Had the Corinthians refused obedience, the apostle would feel that he had lost all authority over them, and that his work at Corinth was ruined. This disastrous issue there was too much reason to apprehend. It was therefore "out of much affliction and anguish of heart, I wrote to you with many tears" (2 Cor. 2:4), that he wrote the sharp reproofs and stern condemnation which we read in 1 Corinthians 4—6. If this letter fail to rouse their conscience and bring them to order and right feeling, he must count the Corinthian church as lost; he will be himself bereaved of children who, with all their faults, were very dear to him, and a blow will be inflicted on the kingdom of Christ, the more severe because of the number and extraordinary gifts of this community, and because of the unique position of Corinth as the capital of Greece and the steppingstone from east to west, from Antioch to Rome.

Looking at matters in this light, we can enter into the conflicting emotions under which the apostle wrote this letter and the anxiety with which he awaited its result, as they appear from his subsequent references in 2 Corinthians 2:4, 12, 13; 7:5–9. When the danger was over, he allowed expression, in the second epistle, to these feelings of distress. In the first epistle he bears himself with perfect self-control, with the calm and firm courage of the pilot at the height of the storm. First Corinthians 5 was, in effect, *Paul's ultimatum to Corinth*.

Character and Scope of the Epistle

There are two important links between the Thessalonian and first Corinthian epistles: the subject of *the parousia* (cf. 1 Cor. 15; 1 Thess.

4:13–18) and that of *the sanctity of the body* (cf. 1 Cor. 6:12–20 with
1 Thess. 4:1–8). But in passing from those letters to this we are
conscious of a great enlargement of our field of view. The Thessalonians were like men fighting their way through some defile amidst a
host of enemies, who see only at the end of the pass the sky before
them bright with the coming of their Savior. But now we have issued
into a wider region. The dawn of Christ's advent still shines in the
heaven, and hope counts "the time" but "shortened" till His appearing (1 Cor. 7:29). Yet, if short, it is a time of eager and manifold
activity, and the scene is one in which the powers and passions of
human life are brought into full play.

Among the great provincial cities of the Empire, Corinth was the
most central and was affected by all the various currents of the age.
Standing on Grecian soil, it was a Roman colony, refounded by
Julius Caesar in 46 B.C., the seat of Roman government and of
Greek commerce. For profligacy this city had an infamous notoriety.
Here vice was raised into a religion, and the "idolaters" of Corinth
are fitly set between "fornicators" and "adulterers" (1 Cor. 6:9).
From the filthiest slough of sin Paul's converts at Corinth were ex-
tracted (1 Cor. 6:9–11). Not even at Antioch had he seen the condition of the Gentile world—its pride and power, its fancied wisdom,
its utter depravity and godlessness—displayed so vividly. It was
from Corinth that he wrote the first chapter of the epistle to the Romans, describing what was there before his eyes. At first, we can imagine, he was staggered by the awful wickedness of Corinth. To this,
along with other causes, we may attribute the "in weakness and in
fear and in much trembling" in which his ministry there commenced (1 Cor. 2:3).

It was under these circumstances, contemplating human guilt in
its extreme and most revolting form, that the sacrifice of Christ revealed itself to him with new power as the all-sufficient remedy for sin.
He marks his arrival at Corinth as an event in his history, the occasion of a memorable resolve: "I determined to know nothing among
you except Jesus Christ, and Him crucified" (1 Cor. 2:2). The temptation may have come to him at Athens, and among "the Greeks"
that "seek after wisdom," to adopt a more philosophical style of
teaching, such as that in which Apollos afterwards excelled, but if
such thoughts did occur, he put them quickly aside and determined

now more than ever to make the cross the center of his aims, the glory and power of all his ministry to sinful men.

Central Principle of the Epistle

In "the word of the cross" (1 Cor. 1:17, 18) we find the principle which underlies the teaching of this epistle and binds together its varied and divergent topics. From that fountain, now opened for the apostle's mind to its very depths, flows the rich and powerful stream of thought that pours through these pages. The word (or doctrine) of the cross includes, of course, that of the resurrection, of the new life and the believer's mystic union with Christ crucified and risen—in fact, the entire theology which the apostle is about to expound in writing to the Romans, which is all conveyed by implication here. It is, in truth, from the summit of Calvary that the many subjects are considered which come under review in 1 and 2 Corinthians. In the piercing light of the cross the manifold problems of life are surveyed. Greek wisdom and Corinthian vice, church parties, spiritual gifts and their abuse, great social questions such as marriage and slavery, lighter matters of diet and of dress, all are discussed in their bearing on the relationship of men to Christ and upon principles deduced from the word of the cross.

In this we recognize the characteristic mark of this book of the New Testament. It is *the epistle of the doctrine of the cross in application.* Among the four evangelical epistles it holds a place in the practical sphere similar to that of Romans in the theoretical and theological. In the latter writing the apostle does but reason out and demonstrate the principle on which he has already acted with success in dealing with the ethical problems and violent conflicts of the church at Corinth. In the practical world the gospel begins by winning its decisive victories, which are then completed in the region of theory and scientific doctrine. It gives *life* first, then the philosophy of life. In 1 Corinthians it proves itself the "power of God"; in Romans it will prove itself equally "God's wisdom." This order is the reverse of what we might anticipate, but it is God's way, and the order of salvation.

Besides the special difficulties arising from the state of the Corinthian church—from its party strife, its intellectual pride and love of display, and its laxity of conscience in regard to sexual sin—there

were other questions, belonging to the new Christian society at
large, which emerged in the active life of this church and called for
settlement at this juncture; questions partly internal to the church and
arising from the communion of Jews and Gentiles within it, partly arising from the contact of Christians with heathen or Jewish society outside. There was, for example, the dispute as to the lawfulness of
eating flesh that had been offered in sacrifice to idols and of sitting at
the table of idolaters; the propriety of resorting to heathen tribunals;
the moral value of celibacy; the place of women in Christian assem-
blies; the rule of expediency in the use of things lawful; the relative
worth of the various kinds of spiritual gifts. These matters, some of
them of the most delicate and controversial nature, are treated with
admirable penetration and good sense, in a manner calculated to impress the intelligent Corinthians with profound respect for the apostle's wisdom. But it is the doctrine of the cross from which he draws
this wisdom. Here is "the master light of all his seeing." From it he
learns the subservience of the material to the spiritual, and its glori-
fication by the spiritual. The sacrifice of Christ supplies the power by
which knowledge is yoked to the service of love, and selfish instincts are subordinated to the common good. The well-being of
society, the right ordering of all human affairs, lies in the application
of these principles, of which Paul, next to Jesus Christ, is our greatest teacher. This epistle furnishes lessons in the doctrine of the cross
that are of universal import and apposite to the needs of every age.

Analysis of the Epistle

This epistle, we must remember, is a thoroughly practical one. Its topics were supplied by the defects and disorders of the Corinthian
church. These are known to the apostle from two sources: (1)
Through *the letter lately sent to him by the church.* To this he expressly
replies in 1 Corinthians 7:1, and probably the matters taken up in succession in 1 Corinthians 8:1, 12:1, 16:1, all introduced in similar fashion, were brought before the apostle by the epistle of the church. From
this letter we conjecture that Paul is quoting in 1 Corinthians 11:2,
where he says, "Now I praise you because you remember me in
everything, and hold firmly to the traditions, just as I delivered
them to you." In view of what follows and of the general tenor of the

epistle, we can hardly account for such a commendation otherwise. First Corinthians 5:2 expressly says that the Corinthians were too well pleased with themselves, and the irony of 1 Corinthians 4:8–10, 17, shows that they did *not* sufficiently remember Paul's "ways which are in Christ."

The epistle is further based (2) on *reports Paul had received*, outside the above letter, *of the state of things at Corinth*. First Corinthians 1—6 deal mainly with these matters of report; 1 Corinthians 7—16, as we suppose, with the questions raised in the aforesaid letter. There are later allusions to the damaging reports in 1 Corinthians 11:18; probably also in 1 Corinthians 15:12, 33, 34, and elsewhere. From his own recent visit (to which, however, he makes no open reference), and from information supplied by Apollos who had crossed over to Ephesus shortly before, Paul would gather additional material for this letter.

The epistle being thus altogether objective and the product of the occasion, is of a desultory character. It does not lend itself readily to analysis. We divide it into the following sections:

Salutation, and Thanksgiving, 1 Corinthians 1:1–9.

Paul gives thanks for *the rich spiritual endowments* of this church, and declares his confidence that *God will perfect the work of grace* in them.

§ 1. Concerning *the divisions*, 1 Corinthians 1:10—4:21:

especially that between the self-styled *parties of Paul and Apollos, and* its causes, lying in fondness for eloquence and affectation of philosophy. Hence Paul denounces (not in Apollos, but in his followers): (1) *wisdom of words*, in contrast with the divine folly of the cross, 1 Corinthians 1:18—2:16, and (2) *glorying in men*, by contrast with glorying in the Lord, 1 Corinthians 3, 4. Throughout this reproof there runs (3) a continuous *vindication* by the apostle *of his own method* as a Christian teacher, *and his claims* on the Corinthians as their spiritual father.

§ 2. Concerning *the case of incest*, 1 Corinthians 5; 6:12–20:

(1) He bids the offender be "deliver[ed]" for bodily punishment "to Satan," and this foul "leaven" purged out of the church, 1 Corinthians 5:1–8. 2) He repeats more distinctly his former direction to excommunicate immoral persons, 1 Corinthians 5:9–13. (3) He returns, in 1 Corinthians 6:12–20, to the subject of sexual sin; distinguishing between questions of

expediency such as that of "meats," and those of *fundamental morals* such as that of "fornication," against which he launches a solemn interdict.

§ 3. Concerning *the use by Christians of heathen law-courts*, 1 Corinthians 6:1–11:

From the connection in which this matter is introduced, it appears to have been mixed up with the last. Probably the affairs of the family polluted by the crime just referred to, had in some way come before the civil magistrates.

§ 4. Concerning *the expedience of celibacy*, 1 Corinthians 7:

Here we must distinguish between *advice* and *command*, also between that which belongs to universal Christian law and what was dictated by the circumstances of the time. In 1 Corinthians 7:17–24 reference is made to other callings in life besides marriage, especially the state of *slavery*.

§ 5. Concerning *meats offered to idols*, 1 Corinthians 8—10:

A thorny subject, touching the social life of the church in various ways. The apostle says (1) that the difficulty is to be solved by *love*, not by mere knowledge, 1 Corinthians 8. (2) He brings to bear upon it *his own example* in matters morally indifferent, 1 Corinthians 9, intimating that in theory he was for freedom, but in practice for self-denying strictness. (3) He warns the Corinthians against idolatrous feasts:

(*a*) by *the history of ancient Israel*, in 1 Corinthians 10:1–14;

(*b*) *the sacredness of the Lord's supper*, 1 Corinthians 10:15–22.

(4) Explicit directions on the subject follow, in 1 Corinthians 10:23—11:1.

§ 6. Concerning certain *disorders in public worship*, 1 Corinthians 11:2–34:

(1) The decorous *behavior of women*, 1 Corinthians 11:2–16; (2) *the profanation of the Lord's supper*, whose origin and spiritual import he sets forth in 1 Corinthians 11:17–34.

§ 7. Concerning *the exercise of spiritual gifts*, 1 Corinthians 12—14:

(1) The *nature of these manifold gifts* is set forth, and their varied use illustrated, by the figure of *the body and its members*, 1 Corinthians 12. (2) *Prophecy is extolled* as superior in usefulness to the more admired gift of tongues, 1 Corinthians 14:1–25. (3) Directions given for their, *orderly and seemly exercise* in the church-meetings, 1 Corinthians 14:26–40. (4) In the midst of this section the apostle delivers, by the way, his wonderful *encomium upon love* (or *charity*), which he exalts above all miraculous gifts, above knowledge, and even above faith and hope, 1 Corinthians 13.

§ 8. Concerning *the resurrection of the body*, 1 Corinthians 15:

This subject the apostle has reserved till the last. He discusses it with fullness and solemnity, discerning in the speculative unbelief that had arisen at Corinth respecting it a new and profound peril to the Christian faith. This is the one expressly doctrinal section of the epistle. It has no direct connection with the foregoing topics (but see 1 Cor. 6:13, 14). Paul shows: (1) that denial of bodily resurrection involves denial of *Christ's resurrection*, and so contradicts and stultifies the gospel, 1 Corinthians 15:1–19. (2) That Christ's resurrection is the pledge of *the victory of God's kingdom*, and the warrant of the believer's hope in Him, 1 Corinthians 15:20–34. (3) That the principle of the resurrection *runs through Nature*, from the death of the seed a higher life being unfolded, 1 Corinthians 15:35–49. (4) Finally, it is revealed that *Christ's advent* will bring about the resurrection of the departed and the transformation of living saints, alike necessary for their entrance into the final kingdom of God, of which the Corinthians must cherish an unwavering hope, 1 Corinthians 15:50–58.

The Conclusion, 1 Corinthians 16:

Touching the collection for Jerusalem, the apostle's plans of travel, the sending of Timothy to Corinth, the arrival of Stephanas and his companions; followed by brief exhortations and greetings, an anathema on those who "do not love not the Lord," an invocation of Christ's grace, and a final assurance of the apostle's *love to all*.

We will add, as before, a paraphrase of some of the salient passages of the epistle:

First Corinthians 4:6–9: "Now, I have applied all this (1 Cor. 3:4—4:5) to the case of Apollos and myself for your benefit, hoping that by this example you will learn to keep your thoughts concerning men within the rule of Scripture (see 1 Cor. 1:31, 2:16, 3:19–21), and will cease to pride yourselves on belonging to one leader in contempt of another. If you differ from others, who is it makes the difference? What have you, pray, that you did not receive? If you received it, why boast of it as though it were your own?

"And how much you have received! enough, it seems, and more than enough already! You have grown rich, forsooth; you have come into your kingdom, and need us no longer! Aye, would to God that you were kings indeed; that we, too, might share your royalty! As for us the apostles, it seems to me that God has set us in the last place, as men condemned to death and kept for the end of the show. We have become a spectacle to the whole world, alike to angels and to men!"

First Corinthians 6:12–20: " 'All things are lawful,' say you? Yes, but not all things are profitable. All things are lawful for me (are in my power), but I will not be brought under the power of any. Foods, for example, are for the belly, and the belly for its foods; both of them God will abolish. Not so with the body: it is not for fornication (the maxim 'All things are lawful' has no place here); it belongs to the Lord, and the Lord to it, and God who raised up the Lord Jesus will raise us from the dead also through His power.

"Do you not know that your bodies are limbs of Christ? Shall I then take Christ's limbs away from Him, and make them limbs of a harlot? The thought is monstrous! The man who attaches himself to a harlot, is, as you know, one body with her: according to what Scripture says of the union of man and woman, 'The two shall be one flesh.' So, on the other hand, he who attaches himself to the Lord is one spirit with Him.

"Flee from fornication. Every other act of sin a man may commit, lies outside the body, but the fornicator sins against his own body. Do you not know that your body is a temple of the Holy Spirit within you, the Spirit you have from God, and that you are not your own property? You were *bought*, with what a price! Glorify God, then, in your body."

First Corinthians 10:23–30: " 'All things are lawful.' Very good, but not all things are profitable. 'All things are lawful,' but not all things are edifying. Let no one seek his own advantage, but every one his fellow's.

"You may eat anything that is sold in the market, with a good conscience, asking no questions about it, for 'The earth, with its fullness, is the Lord's.' If anyone who is not a Christian asks you to dinner and you are minded to go, eat whatever is set before you, with a good conscience, asking no questions about it. But supposing someone should say, 'Now, this meat was killed in sacrifice!' eat no more of it, for the sake of him that told you, and for conscience' sake, I mean the conscience of the other, not your own. For it is not well that my liberty should be condemned by another man's conscience, and that, while I am partaking with thankfulness to God, in the midst of my thanksgiving I should be reviled for this very thing!"

First Corinthians 15:12–19: "Now, if Christ is preached and the fact of His resurrection, how is it that some of you can say, 'There is no resurrection of the dead'? If that is the case, why then *Christ* has not been raised, and if Christ has not been raised, the gospel we preached, and your faith in it, are empty and vain. Yes, and we are proved to be false witnesses towards God, for we have borne witness, to God's discredit, that He raised up the Christ, when He did nothing of the kind, if it is true that the dead never rise. For if the dead do not rise, Christ has not risen.

"Moreover, if Christ has not risen, your faith is useless: you are still in your sins. Then, too, it follows that those who fell asleep in Christ perished! If the hope we have cherished in Christ ends with this life, we of all men are most to be pitied."

First Corinthians 15:44–49: "If there is a natural body (one that suits the soul as it is), there is also a spiritual body. And thus it stands written: 'The first man, that is, Adam, became a living soul,' while the last Adam became a life-giving spirit. It is the natural (that which belongs to the soul) which comes first, not the spiritual: this must follow. The first man comes of the earth, and is earthy: the second man is from heaven. These two have each his counterpart, in earthy and in heavenly men. And even as we have worn the image of the earthy (Adam), we are also to wear the image of the heavenly (Christ)."

Additional Note: Since writing the above, the author has come to a somewhat different opinion on two connected points, noticed on pages 43, 44, 47, namely, on the visit of Timothy to Corinth and the letter to Corinth referred to in 2 Corinthians 2 and 7. He can no longer account for the allusions of 2 Corinthians 2:4–11; 7:8–12 by what is contained in 1 Corinthians, nor identify the Corinthian that "caused sorrow" (2 Cor. 2:5) and "offended" (2 Cor. 7:12) of 2 Corinthians with the "such a one" of 1 Corinthians 5:1–5, making him "the one offended" (2 Cor. 7:12) the same as the injured "father" of 1 Corinthians 5:1. The tone of feeling and turn of expression marked in 2 Corinthains 2 and 7 point to this "wrong" as having consisted in some gross affront put upon the apostle about which he was compelled to write "out much affliction" and "with anguish of heart," in the interval between the extant epistles, a letter carried by Titus to Corinth, which led to the "punishment" by the vote of the church of the insolent offender and the "repentance" on the church's part de-scribed in 2 Corinthians 2. This insult (reproved by letter) had been suffered not by the apostle in person, but probably through Timothy, who, on this supposition, reached Corinth soon after the arrival of 1 Corinthians (see 16:10, 11) and represented Paul in that unruly church. See, further, the article Paul in Hastings' Dictionary of the Bible, volume 3.

The Second to the
Corinthians

Interval Between 1 and 2 Corinthians.

Paul's departure from Ephesus was hastened by the tumult raised by the shrine-makers of Artemis (or Diana) against him (Acts 19:21—20:1). It was some time before Pentecost, in the year 56, when "he departed to go to Macedonia." He journeyed to Troas, awaiting there the return of Titus from Corinth before he should embark for Macedonia, and making use of the "door . . . opened" to him at this place to preach Christ (2 Cor. 2:12, 13). Accordingly, we find a Pauline church in existence at Troas on the apostle's return journey this way in the following spring (Acts 20:6–12). But Titus did not arrive at the time expected, and the apostle finding "no rest for [his] spirit" on this account, oppressed with anxiety about the church of Corinth, bade farewell to his new friends at Troas and pushed on to meet Titus in Macedonia.

This was the darkest hour in Paul's life, since the days he spent in blindness at Damascus. Referring to it again in 2 Corinthians 7:5, he writes: "For even when we came into Macedonia, our flesh had no rest, but we were afflicted on every side: conflicts without, fears within." Corinth appeared to be in full revolt against him. Galatia was falling away to "another gospel." He had narrowly escaped with his life from the enraged populace of Ephesus, "wild beasts" with whom he had long been fighting and at whose mercy he had left his flock in that turbulent city (1 Cor. 15:32). He was "burdened excessively, beyond our strength." Under this continued strain of excitement and anxiety, his strength succumbed; he was seized with an attack of sickness which threatened to terminate his life. "We despaired even of life," he says: "we had the sentence of death within ourselves" (2 Cor. 1:8, 9).

This last expression, combined with the language of 2 Corinthians 4:7—5:4 ("this treasure in earthen vessels . . . carrying about in the body the dying of Jesus . . . though our outer man is decaying," etc.), appears to us to intimate very clearly that, in referring to "our affliction which came to us in Asia" and which proved so nearly fatal, the apostle is thinking not so much of the danger incurred by persecution as of his enfeebled physical condition. He had been at death's door. His life and work, to all appearance, were coming to an end, and under circumstances of the most ominous nature. Together with his life the fate of his mission and of Gentile Christianity trembled in the balance. Never had he felt himself so helpless, so beaten down and discomfited, as on that melancholy journey from Ephesus to Macedonia and while he lay upon his sick-bed (perhaps at Philippi), knowing not whether Titus or the messenger of death would reach him first.

This crisis left a deep mark on Paul's spiritual history. First Corinthians 4:7—5:9 is a leaf from his autobiography. It is a record of his inner experience during this sorrowful period. For the first time since he became a believer in Jesus Christ, he has realized the fact that he may not hope within his own lifetime to see the Lord return in glory. He must be "absent from the body . . . to be at home with the Lord." And to this he consents, not without a struggle, for he shrank from the bitterness of death. "We do not want," he writes, "to be unclothed, but to be clothed [to put on the heavenly body above the earthly, absorbing and superseding it], in order that what is mortal may be swallowed up by life" (2 Cor. 5:4). But if this may not be, still he is "always confident." "We know," he says, "that if the earthly tent, which is our house is torn down, we have a building from God, a house not made with hands, eternal in the heavens" (2 Cor. 5:1)! So the apostle, in this faith, has encountered and overcome for himself the king of terrors. From this time forward he expected, as he puts it in Philippians 1:23, to "*depart* and be with Christ," and this was his personal desire. Never subsequently does he write, as he did in 1 Thessalonians 4:15, 17 and 1 Corinthians 15:51, of those who should be found living at the Lord's Second Coming in the *first person*. We must not be surprised at a change of view upon this point, for even apostles only "knew" and "prophesied in part." Christ spoke of a speedy coming, but forbade all attempts to fix the time beforehand. Until otherwise instructed, it was the more reverent and natural thing for the church in the apostolic age to expect Him at any time, and its language necessarily reflected this feeling and desire.

The expectation of the *parousia* had been so powerful in its influence upon the apostle's mind that the lesson and the revelation he now received necessarily made a considerable difference to him and affected his teaching in various directions. A longer perspective of earthly life and warfare for the church opens before his eyes (Rom. 1:5, 16:26; Eph. 2:7). Family relationships and civil duties resume their importance. We find the relation of Christ and His kingdom to nature and material things interesting the apostle's mind in subsequent epistles, in a way that was scarcely possible while the return of the Lord Jesus and the end of the existing world occupied the immediate foreground of his field of view. Brief, then, as the interval was that separated the first and second epistles to the Corinthians, it was a memorable epoch and a turning-point in the apostle's life and the course of his thoughts. He rose from his sick-bed with a serene and lofty spirit, master of the fears within and assured that he would prevail in the fightings that had well-nigh overwhelmed him from without. Titus returned with news from Corinth which re-established his shattered health more quickly than all the medicines in the world.

Titus' Report from Corinth

The relief which Paul now experienced was as intense as had been the previous distress and alarm into which he was plunged by the misconduct of the Corinthians. "But God, who comforts the depressed, comforted us by the coming of Titus. . . . he reported to us your longing, your mourning, your zeal for me. . . . For behold what earnestness this very thing, this godly sorrow, has produced in you; what vindication of yourselves, what indignation, what fear, what longing, what zeal, what avenging of wrong! . . . Great is my confidence in you, great is my boasting on your behalf; I am filled with comfort. I am overflowing with joy (2 Cor. 7:4) . . . I rejoice that in everything I have confidence in you" (2 Cor. 7:6–16). Evidently, previous epistles had brought about a reaction in the church of Corinth; there had been an outburst of loyalty towards the apostle and indignation and repugnance against the chief offender, who had treated Paul's authority with insolent and for the time successful defiance.

The sentence which the apostle required the church to pass upon this conspicuous transgressor had been inflicted by the general vote (2 Cor. 2:5–7), with an emphasis that left nothing to be desired. Under this condemnation, and the heavy penalties involved in it, the stubborn offender had quailed. He made haste to repent of his sin, and was now so changed and humbled that the apostle sees fit in writing again to intercede for him, and even intreats the church to restore its love to the unhappy man. On the two main matters of dispute, his apprehensions are therefore relieved. It is clear that the majority of the Corinthian church will no longer tolerate flagrant impurity in their midst, and are loyal to himself as their father in Christ. (See, however, Note on pp. 55, 56.)

The majority, we say, for this is what the words of 2 Corinthians 2:6 signify, "this punishment which was inflicted by *the majority*." It is to the faithful majority, which had rallied to the apostle's side and inflicted a crushing reproof on the object of his condemnation, that Paul's "mouth has spoken freely" and his "heart is opened wide" (2 Cor. 6:11). By them "Titus' spirit had been refreshed," and Paul's "glorying" in them justified. And in them he now rejoices with a renewed and full confidence. But a majority implies *a minority*. Some had not concurred in the vote of excommunication. And the latter part of the epistle shows that Paul had still enemies at Corinth, of the most dangerous and virulent character. Indeed, there is much more of the language of denunciation in this letter than in the former. The four parties that were distinguishable when the first epistle was written, are now resolved into *two*. The Apollonian fraction, marked off from the Pauline by personal attachment and admiration more than by difference of principle, seems to have disappeared. On the other hand, the Petrine party, consisting of those who boasted, "I [am] of Cephas," had grown bolder and more bitter in their antagonism. Judaistic partisans would naturally oppose the claims that Paul had put forward in the first epistle, and the apostolic jurisdiction which he there asserted. Many indications show that the opponents he has in view in 2 Corinthians 10—13 belonged to this faction, and assumed to be supporters of the Twelve and of the mother church at Jerusalem against the pretensions and innovations of Paul.

Quite recently there had arrived at Corinth "certain persons" with "letters of commendation" (2 Cor. 3:1), obtained in all probability from Jerusalem (cf. Acts 15:1, 24; Gal. 2:12), whose presence goes far to account for the new situation now disclosed at Corinth and for the manner in which the apostle vindicates himself in the latter part of this epistle. These men professed to represent the true apostles of Jesus Christ; Paul, they said, stood far behind them (2 Cor. 11:5, 12:11). They claimed, indeed, to be themselves "apostles of Christ" with a right as good as that which he could assert (2 Cor. 11:13). They accused him of arrogance and unmeasured boasting (2 Cor. 10:8–18); they ridiculed his person and speech, and alleged that he was bold only by letter and from a distance (2 Cor. 10:1, 2, 10; 13:10). In his humble demeanor and his refusal to take payment for his work they saw a hidden craft, and at the same time a tacit confession of his inferiority (2 Cor. 11:7–12; 12:13–18). For their own part, they supported their dignity by large exactions (2 Cor. 11:12, 20, 21; 12:13), for they belonged to the "Hebrew" aristocracy, and were of the true and legitimate ministers of Christ (2 Cor. 11:22, 23). They spoke of visions and revelations, moreover, and of other "signs of a true apostle," in regard to which they set Paul below themselves (2 Cor. 12:1, 12), and they said that churches which acknowledged such a man for their chief must be content to remain in an inferior and secondary position, as compared with those founded and directly governed by the original apostles (2 Cor. 12:13). Throughout Paul is combating a systematic and cunning attempt to overthrow his authority at Corinth, in which the Judean emissaries took the lead, supported by a minority in the church. By these men he was attacked openly, and with the most malicious weapons. They aimed at nothing short of his deposition from the apostleship, and at bringing the churches founded by Paul under the direction of Jerusalem.

In Galatia, as we shall afterwards find, the Judaistic agitators denounced Paul's doctrine, while they seem to have spared his person, but at Corinth the assault was mainly of a personal character. In each case the ground of conflict was skillfully chosen. For the Galatian converts had been warmly attached to the apostle, but probably entered with less intelligence and sympathy into his teaching. The Corinthian church, on the other hand, was distinguished for its intellectual gifts, for its breadth of mind and love of liberty, but it displayed less personal devotion to Paul, and its contentious disposition laid it open to the arts of his maligners. The recent strife within this church, and the high tone of authority that Paul assumed on the question of discipline, gave them a vantage ground of which they made the utmost use. From 2 Corinthians 11:3, 4 it appears, however, that the doctrinal question was involved along with the personal, and lay in reality behind it. It was "another Jesus . . . a different spirit . . . a different gospel" that was being introduced and preached, under cover of the disparagement and insult heaped upon the apostle Paul.

We have now accounted for the two chief sections of the epistle, based as it was upon the report of Titus. It remains to add that *the collection for Jerusalem*, which "Achaia" had declared itself "prepared" to make "since last year" (2 Cor. 9:2), and about which particular instructions were given in the first epistle, had not yet been completed at Corinth. So Paul addresses himself to the subject once more, in 2 Corinthians 8—9, notifying at the same time the return of Titus to Corinth to conclude this business; along with whom a representative of Macedonia is sent, a brother of high repute among the churches (2 Cor. 8:6, 16–24), very possibly the evangelist Luke.

Characteristics of 2 Corinthians

Let us now endeavor to comprehend the nature of Paul's second epistle to the Corinthians. It differs very greatly from the first, alike in tone and contents. The first is objective and practical; the second intensely subjective and personal. The first is calm and measured in tone, sometimes severe, but always collected and deliberate; the second is broken, vehement, impassioned, now melting to the softest affection, now rising into a storm of indignant reproach and sarcasm. The first epistle reflects the nature of the Corinthian church: its abundance of talent and activity, its truly Greek fractiousness and love of display, its defects of conscience and moral sense, its close relations with heathen society; the second reveals the nature of the apostle Paul himself: his sensitive honor and contempt for chicanery, the tenderness and ardor of his affection for the Gentile churches, the affection of a mother or lover rather than that which commonly belongs to the teacher and the pastor; the frailty of his delicate yet active and enduring frame, the unparalleled hardships he endured, the violent enmities amidst which he moved, his continual sense of eternal things, the supernatural visitations and mystical raptures that he experienced, the awful miraculous powers he was capable of exerting, his absolute sincerity and self-abnegation, his absorbing devotion to the doctrine and message of the cross, all these qualities of the great apostle and characteristics of his work stand out in the pages of this letter with amazing vividness and power. Never has any man painted himself more naturally and more effectively than Paul in the letter before us. To see him at his greatest as a thinker and theologian, we turn to the epistle to the Romans; to know him as a saint, we read the Philippian epistle. But if we would measure him as a man among men, and as a minister of Christ; if we would sound the depths of his heart and realize the force and fire of his nature, the ascendancy of his genius and the charm of his manner and disposition, we must thoroughly understand the second letter to the Corinthians.

This is Paul's *apologia pro vita sua*. Its main interest is not doctrinal, as in Galatians and Romans, although there are weighty passages of doctrine in it, nor practical, as in 1 Corinthians and the Pastorals, although 2 Corinthians 8 and 9 in the middle of the letter are practical enough: it is intensely personal, made up of explanation, defense, protestation, appeal, reproach, invective, threatening, with a vein of subduing pathos blended with the most subtle irony running through the whole. Paul's heart just now is very tender. He has been down in the gulfs of sorrow, and lying beneath the shadow of death. The restored affection of the Corinthian church found him in the state when such a cordial was most needed, and it moved his whole nature in response; while the insolence and intrigues of the Judaists, now disclosed in their full baseness, roused in him a scorn that knew no bounds and a triumphant confidence in the "weapons of" his apostolic "warfare" and in his power "for the destruction of" their "fortresses" (2 Cor. 10:1–6).

The epistle is written, therefore, in a strain of keen and high emotion. There runs through it a peculiar mental tension, such as prolonged and deep suffering leaves behind it in a nature like Paul's, which we shall find continued in the epistle to the Galatians. It bears visibly "the brand-marks of Jesus"(Gal. 6:17; cf. 2 Cor. 4:10) impressed on the apostle's spirit no less than on his body. Its emotional nature makes the dissection of the writing difficult, and impossible to carry into detail. Feeling cannot be reduced to system and laid out in cold analysis; it vanishes under the dissecting knife. Again and again, when we seem to be on the track of some regular sequence of thought, the spring of emotion is touched and it surges up in a tide that carries grammar and logic away with it and sets at defiance our schemes of analysis. This disconnectedness has led some critics, very needlessly, to question the unity of the epistle. Feeling has, after all, a logic of its own. With this caution, and careful not to attempt too much, we will proceed with our analysis.

Analysis of 2 Corinthians

The epistle consists of two distinct apologies, with a homily on the collection for Jerusalem interjected between them.

A. The apostle's *defense of his ministry before the Corinthian church.* Second Corinthians 1—7

§ 1. Introduced (after the salutation) by a thanksgiving for *the comfort that attended his recent troubles* (2 Cor. 1:3, 7), and an account of *the danger he had passed through* (2 Cor. 1:8–11).

§ 2. *The defense of his conduct in recent occurrences* (2 Cor. 1:12—2:17): especially in regard to the delay of his visit to Corinth, and his disposition toward the man lately subject to discipline there.

§ 3. Touching *the general character and spirit of his ministry* (2 Cor. 3—6): its attitude toward the old covenant (3), its divine origin (2 Cor. 4:1–6), the frailty of its earthly instrument (2 Cor. 4:7–18), its relation to eternal things (2 Cor. 5:1–13), its great message of reconciliation (2 Cor. 5:14—6:2), and the temper in which it is pursued (2 Cor. 6:3–10).

§ 4. This defense is followed by *an appeal* to the Corinthians *for reciprocal affection* (2 Cor. 6:11–13; 7:2, 3), and an account of the impression made upon him by *the tidings which Titus had brought from them* (2 Cor. 7:4–16). (To 2 Cor. 6:14—7:1 we made reference on p. 45.)

B. The *homily on the collection.* Second Corinthians 8, 9.

These two chapters are so different in purport and tone from the rest of the letter that some critics suppose them to be foreign to it and think they were imported into this place from another source, but we have seen that the subject demanded a place in this epistle, and the change of tone is in harmony with a nature like Paul's. After the first wave of emotion has spent itself, a quiet, level passage such as this gives relief to the readers, while it serves an important purpose of its own. Then it is followed by another outburst, still more animated than the first. The reader may judge for himself how much the effect of the second apology (2 Cor. 10—13) is heightened by this pause and interlude, and how skillfully it diverts the attention, otherwise overstrained.

In these two chapters the apostle gives an account of what had been done, and remained to be done, in this matter: he acknowledges the hearty interest the Corinthians had shown in it, and reminds them of the Christian motives bearing upon the work, "the grace of our Lord Jesus Christ" (2 Cor. 8:9), the blessedness of the generous giver (2 Cor. 9:6–11), and the thanksgiving which their bounty would cause to redound to God (2 Cor. 9:12–15).

C. The apostle's *vindication of himself against his adversaries at Corinth.* Second Corinthians 10—13

In the former apology (2 Cor. 1—6) Paul had in view the Corinthian church at large, now chastened and at amity with himself; in the latter he is dealing with a particular class of rancorous personal enemies: "some," he says, "who regard us as if we walked according to flesh," men who denied his office, who despised his authority, and who poured contempt on his person and his teaching, who made Paul and his apostleship the mark of their attacks in order to overthrow the doctrine that he preached and establish "a different gospel." Hence the striking change of tone in this section, a change from gentleness to severity, from entreaty to invective, from the warmth of love to that of indignation.

§ 1. In 2 Corinthians 10, and again more categorically in 2 Corinthians 13, the apostle *asserts his authority,* and declares his intention to use it unsparingly at Corinth, should it still be needful. He will show, indeed, that he can act as vigorously as he writes.

§ 2. In 2 Corinthians 11:1–15, and again in 2 Corinthians 12:14–21, he *denounces his slanderers* and *exposes their misrepresentations.*

§ 3. In 2 Corinthians 11:16—12:13, he *compares himself with them,* especially in respect of his sufferings and the revelations he had received.

The Conclusion (2 Cor. 13:11–13) breathe words full of peace and kindness. It is the sudden lull with which the storm dies down at the close of day.

Paraphrases of Select Passages

Second Corinthians 2:5–11: "But if anyone has caused grief, it is not myself that he has grieved, but in some degree, for I would not impute too much to him, he has grieved and injured you all. For such a man the reproof inflicted by the vote of the majority is punishment enough. Instead of imposing any further penalty, I would have you forgive him rather and encourage him, lest excess of grief should drive him to despair. Now is the time to renew your love to him. I wrote as I did before not out of desire for the man's punishment, but to try the extent of your loyalty. But if you forgive, then I forgive too. For indeed in what I have forgiven, if I had anything to forgive, I did it on your account, acting in the presence of Christ, and with a fear lest Satan should gain advantage of us, for we know something of his purposes."

Second Corinthians 4:16—5:4: "And so we do not lose heart. While the outer man decays, the inner man is day by day renewed. For our affliction, a light and momentary thing, yields us an eternal glory which immeasurably outweighs it, when we look away from the things that are seen to those unseen. The seen lasts only for a time; the unseen, forever!

"For we know that if our earthly house, this tent in which we dwell, be taken down, we have another house built by God and not of men's handiwork, a house that endures forever in the heavens. In this present habitation, to be sure, we groan and long for our heavenly dwelling, which we would fain put on above it (cf. 1 Cor. 15:52–54), if, indeed, when we put it on, we shall be found still in our bodily dress. We that live in this tent-dwelling, groan under its burdens. Not that we wish to put off the present body, but to put on over it that other dress, and so to have the mortal in us absorbed in the element of life!"

Second Corinthians 6:11–13; 7:2–4: "We write to you, Corinthians, without reserve; we have opened to you all our hearts! If there is any narrowness or coldness, it is not in us; it is in your own feelings. Will you not meet our affection, I speak as to my children, with a like openness toward us? . . . Make room for us within your hearts. There is none of you that we have wronged or injured, or taken advantage of. I do not say this to condemn you, for, as I have said already, you are in our hearts, joined with us for life or death. Great is my freedom in addressing you, great my boasting over you. Nothing could more encourage me, nothing has so filled my heart with joy amidst my troubles as the news which I now hear from Corinth."

Second Corinthians 10:1–6: "Now by the meekness and mildness of Christ I appeal to you, I Paul, the man so lowly among you and to your face, so bold, to be sure, at a distance! I beg of you not to compel me to be bold when I come to you, with the confidence in which I count on being bold against some persons, who account of us as though we walked according to flesh (acting on mere human and sensuous principles). It is true that we walk in the flesh (living in the body), but we do not war after the flesh (contending with bodily weapons against material forces), for our weapons of war are not fleshly, but mighty to do God's work in the overthrow of strongholds, overthrowing hostile arguments and every proud thing that exalts itself against the knowledge of God, and making every human thought and purpose captive to the obedience of Christ. Thus we are ready to punish all disobedience to His rule, so soon as your obedience is made complete."

Second Corinthians 12:19—13:6: "You have been thinking all this time that we are defending ourselves to *you*. Nay, rather, we speak before God in the Spirit of Christ, and it is your edification that we seek in everything. For my fear is lest at my coming I should find you, and you in turn should find me, other than we could wish; lest, perchance, I should find strife and faction raging in all their hateful forms; lest, when I come, my God should once more humble me in regard to you, and I should have to mourn over many of those who had sinned at that former time and have not yet repented of their unchaste and wanton deeds.

"It is now the third time that I am coming to you. 'On the evidence of two or three witnesses a matter shall be confirmed' (Deut. 19:15). What I have already said when with you that second time, I now repeat beforehand: present or absent, I declare to those former sinners, and to all others, that if I come again I will not spare them. For you want a proof, it seems, of the Christ who speaks in me, although He is not weak toward you, but is mighty among you! For if the cross proves Him weak, yet He lives by God's power, and that weakness of His we also share, yet we shall live with Him by God's power, and live for you. It is yourselves, not us, that you need to prove as to whether you are in the faith or not. Nay, surely, you know already that Christ Jesus is in you, or else you are reprobate! But I trust that, when the trial comes, you will see that we are not reprobate!"

To the Galatians

Place of the Galatian Epistle

We left the apostle in Macedonia, where he has just recovered from his prostration, and has addressed his second double-edged epistle to Corinth, a message of reconciliation to the loyal majority of the church and a very thunderbolt against the enemies of his gospel. Now, it is precisely in the strain of the concluding part of 2 Corinthians that the epistle to the Galatians begins. Paul has the same enemies in view, alike in east and west, preachers of "a different gospel" and another Christ than the crucified, deniers of his apostleship, "false brethren" and "deceitful workers," who pretend to represent the first apostles of Jesus and the primitive church at Jerusalem as against himself. This epistle assumes a logical and doctrinal character wanting to 2 Corinthians, but there runs through both the same keen and exalted feeling, an emotion at once tender and severe, the same tone of lofty apostolic self-assertion and relentless hostility to the Judaizers, the same vein of passionate remonstrance and crushing sarcasm. These features had scarcely appeared in 1 Corinthians; in Romans they almost disappear again. They characterize the *two middle letters* of this group and mark the height of the Judaistic controversy. We shall find traces of this polemical style—vehement, thorough-going, yet delicate and careful—in the epistles of later times.

While the feeling and temper of 2 Corinthians run over into Galatians, the ideas of this letter are carried forward and fully developed in Romans. In doctrine and argument the two latter epistles stand in the most intimate connection. Romans 1—8 supplies a calm and luminous exposition of the body of doctrine which Galatians 2—5 sketches out in incisive polemical form. Comparison of Galatians 3:6–22 with Romans 4 and of Galatians 4:4–7 with Romans 8:15–17, in particular, suggests most strongly that these writings followed very closely, if not immediately, upon each other. The above are only conspicuous examples out of a multitude of parallel passages running through the greater part of the Galatian epistle.[1] There is no sameness, no mechanical repetition, but the writer's mind is pursuing an identical line of thought: the same questions are raised, and similarly treated; the doctrine of Justification by Faith is the leading subject of each; even the same texts are quoted, and illustrations used. Hence the late Bishop Lightfoot, in disagreement from most earlier interpreters, maintained that this epistle was written between 2 Corinthians and Romans, that is to say, during the latter part of Paul's journey in Macedonia or the earlier part of his sojourn at Corinth, towards the close of the year A.D. 55 (or, as we rather think, 56) Dr. Beet, in his valuable commentary on this epistle, comes to the same conclusion.

There is nothing in the letter itself to fix definitely either the place or time of its composition. From 1:9; 4:13; 5:3, we gather that Paul had now been in Galatia twice; the epistle was, therefore, subsequent to the journey which he took across Asia Minor in setting out on his third missionary tour (Acts 18:22—19:1). And most students are agreed that it belongs to the period of the legalist controversy and to the second group of epistles. The only question is whether it was written from Ephesus and previously to the Corinthian letters—that is, between the autumn of A.D. 53 and spring of 56—or after these other epistles and from Macedonia or Greece, in the close of the latter year. The words "so quickly" of Galatians 1:6 are adduced in favor of the earlier date, as though they signified "so soon after your conversion" or "soon after I left you." But they rather mean "so soon after the temptation came, so readily, and with such little persuasion" (cf. Gal. 5:7–9). It is the *fickleness* of the Galatians that the apostle deplores.

---

1. See Lightfoot's *Commentary* on Galatians (pp. 47–50), for a detailed comparison of the two writings.

An *early* backsliding, such as the contrary view assumes, would not have been a matter of so great wonder as if it had taken place later.

Galatia, like Corinth, had been disturbed by "troublers" imported from Judea, and a considerable interval must be allowed for their coming and the dissemination of their views, and, again, for full information of their arrival and their disastrous success reaching the apostle. So that, on every account, one is inclined to refer the letter to the last rather than to an earlier period of the third missionary tour. Comparison with the other epistles of the group raises this probability almost to a certainty, and enables us to fix the occasion of this letter with confidence. See further the Postscript.

Paul's Connection with Galatia

Acts records the bare fact that Paul, in his second missionary excursion, traversed "the Phrygian and Galatian region" (Acts 16:6), without a word to indicate how long he stayed there, or with what success he preached; except that, in referring to the apostle's second visit, Luke adds the clause "strengthening all the disciples" (Acts 18:23), from which it is evident that he was well aware of the existence of Pauline churches in the Galatian country, although he has given no account of their establishment.

For this we must fall back upon the epistle itself. In Galatians 4:12–15 the apostle refers, in graphic terms, to his arrival among this people. He had become sick upon his journey over the Phrygian mountains. He reached the Galatian border a broken-down traveler, halting here because his strength had given out and he must stay till it was recruited. This he freely confesses: "Because of a bodily illness that I preached the gospel to you the first time" (Gal. 4:13) because, in fact, he was physically unable to proceed. It was not a promising introduction to this strange people. And besides that, there was something in the nature of his malady which tended to excite contempt, even repulsion, in beholders (Gal. 4:14). In spite of all this, the warm-hearted Gauls received him with enthusiasm. Had he been an "angel of God" or "Christ Jesus *Himself*," they could not have shown him greater hospitality. They thought themselves happy indeed that he had become their guest; there was nothing they would not have done for him, even to have "plucked out your eyes and given them to [him]," as they said with a touch of genuine Celtic exaggeration! Weak as he was, he preached to this susceptible people with marvelous impressiveness, his own suffering condition lending emphasis, as we can imagine, to his descriptions of the sufferings of Christ for men (Gal. 3:1; cf. Gal. 6:17 and 2 Cor. 4:10–11; Col. 1:24). The Holy Spirit wrought mightily with the words of the infirm apostle (Gal. 3:2–5, 14; 4:5–7). Many souls were won for Christ, and through the towns and villages of this wide province a number of churches were formed, over which the apostle watched long enough to know that they "were running well" in the new race (Gal. 5:7). All this implies a considerable length of time spent by Paul and his companions in this district, especially when we consider the bodily state in which he arrived, and observe the fact that the Galatians were not gathered, like most Pauline churches, in a single city, but lived scattered over a wide district.

Taking these facts into account, it appears to us impossible that the ground covered by Acts 15:41—18:1 should have been traversed in a single year. Before they reached "the Phrygian and Galatian region," Paul and Silas had visited "Syria and Cilicia, strengthening the churches." Then they "went through the cities" of Lycaonia, evangelized by Barnabas and Paul some years before. This extensive visitation must have occupied them far into the summer, and to suppose that the Galatian along with some Phrygian churches, and after these the Macedonian churches, were founded, and Athens and Corinth reached, all within the year in which Paul set out from Antioch, seems to us out of the question. We have suggested therefore that the missionary band *spent the winter of 49–50 in Galatia*. Here Paul was kindly nursed, and as his strength returned, his ministrations were extended to various parts of the province. On this view we can understand the intimate knowledge that he shows of this outlying people, and the very considerable knowledge of his doctrine which they had acquired, as well as the warm mutual interest created. (See Hastings' *Dictionary of the Bible*, vol. 3, pp.706, 707.)

The apostle, as we have seen, had again traversed Galatia on his way from Antioch to Ephesus (A.D. 53). Concerning this visit, we know only that he was "strengthening all the disciples" (Acts 18:23), and that he saw already symptoms of the same Judaistic tendency of whose force he had just had such a painful experience at Antioch

(Gal. 1:9; 2:11–21; 5:3), and which was afterwards to reach so dangerous a height in this region. Since that time the apostle has been living mostly at Ephesus, and has evidently kept himself well informed of all that has transpired among the Galatians.

Character of the Galatians[2]

These people were of Celtic descent. *Galatian* is synonymous with *Gallic*. They were the relics of a Gaulish invasion which swept over southeastern Europe in the early part of the third century B.C., and poured into Asia Minor. Here the Celtic tribes maintained themselves in independence under their native princes, until a hundred years later they were subdued by the Romans. Their country now formed a province of the Empire. They had retained much of their ancient language and manners; at the same time, they readily acquired Greek culture, and were superior to their neighbors in intelligence. Jews had settled among them in considerable numbers, and had prepared the way of the gospel; it was through their influence that the Judaistic agitation took so strong a hold of these churches. The epistle implies that its readers generally were acquainted with the Old Testament and with Hebrew history, and that they took, moreover, a lively interest in the affairs of the churches of Jerusalem and Antioch.

None of the New Testament churches possess a more strongly marked character. They exhibit the well-known traits of the Celtic nature. They were generous, impulsive, vehement in feeling and language, but vain (Gal. 5:26), fickle, and quarrelsome. Eight out of the fifteen "deeds of the flesh" enumerated in Galatians 5:20, 21, are sins of *strife*. They could hardly be restrained from "biting and devouring one another" (Gal. 5:15). Like their kinsmen at this time in the west of Europe, they were prone to "carousings and drunkenness." They had probably a natural bent toward a scenic and ritualistic type of religion, which made the spirituality of the gospel pall upon their taste and gave to the teaching of the Judaizers its fatal "bewitchment."

---

2. This description assumes that Paul's "Galatians" were of Galatia proper, the northern part of the province of that name. (See the Postscript). (Most of the observations made, however, apply also to the *Phrygians*, the native substratum throughout the province).

The Judaizers in Galatia

The Judean emissaries found therefore in Galatia a soil prepared and favorable to the growth of the tares they came to sow. They ventured to proceed more openly than their fellow-conspirators at Corinth. They declared that Paul's doctrine was fundamentally defective, and unauthorized. They appealed to the practice of Jesus and the Twelve and to the customs of the mother church in Jerusalem. They quoted the Old Testament, and reasoned upon it with skill and effect. They showed that God had made an indelible covenant with Abraham and his seed, sealed by the token of circumcision, and that Christ had not destroyed or set aside, but fulfilled the Law. The children of Abraham retain, therefore, in the new kingdom of God the privileges which He had guaranteed to them, and Gentile believers, if they would become heirs in full title of the ancient promises, must add to their faith circumcision and conform, as far as might be, to the rule and usage of the church in Jerusalem. Such was the line of "persuasion" adopted by the Judaizers in Galatia, so far as we can recover it from the tenor of Paul's counter-argument.

The apostle's adversaries, while sparing him the indignities cast upon him at Corinth, did not fail to intimate that his ministry was of an inferior and secondary order. His knowledge of the gospel, so they said, and his authority to preach it came from Peter and the Twelve, against whom he now dares to measure himself! "James and Cephas and John," they exclaimed, these are the men "reputed to be pillars" of the faith, everywhere through the church (see Gal. 2:9)! This Paul, with his excessive pretensions, is an upstart, a mere novice in Christianity compared to the others. And, besides, he is inconsistent with himself: it is well known that he formerly "preached" the rite of "circumcision," which in Galatia he so bitterly opposes (Gal. 5:11).

In Galatia therefore as at Corinth, the personal and the doctrinal matters under discussion are involved in each other. But here the theological question, which in 2 Corinthians was lying in the shade, comes to the front and presents itself in its full breadth and its momentous import. It occupies the central and largest part of the letter, being pursued through three chapters of the most profound, condensed, and powerful argument ever expressed in writing. These pages are the charter of evangelical faith; they furnish the basis and ground-plan of the theology of salvation.

Analysis of Galatians

The epistle is intensely polemical. It is *a controversial pamphlet* rather than an ordinary letter. The matter of dispute, as we have seen, is twofold: touching (1) Paul's apostleship, and (2) the nature of the gospel, and the sufficiency of faith in Christ for full salvation. This gives us the order of the first two and main parts of the epistle. (3) A third section is added (Gal. 5:13—6:10), of a moral and hortatory nature, partly occasioned by the shortcomings of the Galatians, and partly designed to show that the doctrine of the cross, instead of relaxing the bonds of morality as the legalists alleged, in reality establishes a higher and, at the same time, a really attainable ethical ideal. The third section, therefore, practical as it is, serves to complete the apostle's theoretical defense, for it overthrows the charge of antinomianism, that from the first was keenly urged against it. "Walk by the Spirit, and you will not carry out the desire of the flesh": in these words lies the principle of the new Christian ethics, the method by which a true faith is translated into a pure life.

The letter, therefore, falls into three consecutive and admirably balanced sections, followed by a brief and incisive summary of the whole (Gal. 6:12–17). In point of coherence and logical structure it contrasts with 2 Corinthians, as much as it resembles it in other ways.[3]

Galatians 1:1–10 we may call the PROLOGUE, containing the *address* and *salutation*, expressed in terms already striking the keynote of the epistle, and the *anathema* (in place of thanksgiving) pronounced on perverters of the gospel.

A. THE PERSONAL HISTORY Galatians 1:11—2:21

Paul asserts *his independent and full apostleship*. He does this by a simple recital of historical facts, in which the critical epochs in his apostolic career are briefly set forth:

---

3.   For a full account of the character and scope of the epistle see the writer's commentary on Galatians, in the *Expositor's Bible* (1888), chapter 1.

1. His conversion and original call (Gal. 1:11–17).

2. His early relations to the church of Jerusalem (Gal. 1:18–24).

3. His meeting with the three "pillars" at the conference held on the status of Gentile believers (Gal. 2:1–10).

4. His collision with Cephas at Antioch (Gal. 1:11–21).

This last paragraph forms a natural and effective transition between the personal and doctrinal sections of the epistle.

B. The Doctrinal Polemic Galatians 3:1—5:12

This *polemical exposition of Paul's gospel* has its text and starting point in the last words of Galatians 2: "If righteousness comes through the Law, then Christ died needlessly."

It is not an abstract theological discussion: argument is mingled with entreaty; scriptural exegesis is interrupted by remonstrance and invective. The thought of his "labor" spent on the Galatians "proving vain" awakens in the apostle recollections of the past (Gal. 4:12–20), which supply a moving episode in the argument, heightening its effect on the hearts of the readers. His proof that *Christ has not died in vain, and that righteousness is not through Law*, is drawn:

1. From his readers' reception of the gospel, and experience of its power (Gal. 3:1–5), and

2. From the blessedness of Abraham, father of believers (Gal. 3:6–9); contrasted with the curse imposed by the Law, from which Christ released us (Gal. 3:10–14).

3. He now establishes *the subordination of the Law to the promise* (Gal. 3:15–18). This is the central point of the argument with the Judaizers.

4. He explains *the design of the Law*, as it prepared for the fulfillment of the promise (Gal. 3:19–24).

5. He declares that faith in Christ makes all men sons of God and heirs of Abraham (Gal. 3:25–29).

The argumentative proof is now complete; what remains serves to illustrate and enforce the position already made good.

6. Before Christ's coming, he says, the human race was like an heir in his minority, who is now emancipated (Gal. 4:1–7).

7. Judaistic conformity is, for converted heathen, no advance, but a relapse! (Gal. 4:8–11).

8. (Parenthetical) The apostle speaks of his old friendship with his readers, and his distress about them (Gal. 4:12–20).

9. He resumes by picturing in the allegory of Hagar and Sarah the states of Christian freedom and legal bondage (Gal. 4:21—5:1).

10. Final protest against his readers' circumcision (Gal. 5:2–12).

C. THE ETHICAL APPLICATION Galatians 5:13—6:10

Liberty is the watchword of the new Israel of God. But the flesh is always ready to find in liberty its opportunity for sin. Against this the apostle must guard; in doing so, he wards off the reproach of antinomian teaching. *Liberty is safe, if it be that of love and of the Spirit.*

1. Love is the law of liberty (Gal. 5:13–15).

2. The Spirit victorious over the flesh (Gal. 5:16–26).

In this paragraph the "deeds of the flesh" and the "fruit of the Spirit" are set forth in turn, that the readers may recognize them.

Two brief and more general homilies follow, concerning:

3. Our brother's burden and our own (Gal. 6:1–5);

4. The sowing and reaping of human life (Gal. 6:6–10).

Galatians 6:11–17 form an EPILOGUE to the epistle. Paul takes the pen from his secretary's hand, and in large characters and brief trenchant words he gathers up and drives home the message of the letter, unmasking finally the insincerity of the Judaizers, while he pleads his own loyalty to the cross of Christ which has marked him with its brand of suffering.

Galatians 6:18 is *the concluding Benediction.*

We will paraphrase below some of the more notable and difficult passages of the epistle:

Galatians 2:14–21: "I said to Cephas before the whole church of Antioch: You are a born Jew, and yet conform to Gentile fashion! With what consistency then, do you put the Jewish yoke upon the Gentiles?

"You and I are both of pure Jewish blood, but our birth and works of Law failed to justify us. Only in Christ, and through faith in Him, was deliverance from our guilt to be obtained; we sought and found it here. So seeking salvation, we proved ourselves to be sinners. But did Christ in bringing us to this experience *make us sinners?* Nothing of the kind! On the other hand, I should make myself a sinner, I should fall inevitably into condemnation, if I set up that abandoned Law again!

"In truth, the Law drove me from itself to Christ. It taught me that through Him only could I live to God. Now that I have been crucified with Christ, I do live, or, rather, Christ lives in me, and this very life of mine in the flesh is a life of faith in Him that loved me and gave Himself up for me. I will not stultify the grace of God. If righteousness can be won by Law, why then Christ died for nothing!"

Galatians 3:19–24: "Why, then, the Law? It was superadded to the promise, in order to provoke transgression (cf. Rom. 5:20), until the promise could take effect. It was administered by angels, and conveyed by a mediator (Moses). This implies two (separated) parties, but *God* (who gave the promise) *is one* (and acted therein by and for Himself).

"Are Law and promise then contradictory? By no means! Had the Law been able to give life, it would have made men righteous (and then there would really have been contradiction), but its office was to hold the world fast under the power of sin, till the promise of life through Christ was ripe for its fulfillment."

Galatians 4:12–20: "Will you not, dear Galatian brothers, come down to my Gentile level? Do not think that I am complaining, as though you had done me wrong! You remember in what condition I first came to you, and I remember well the kindness that you lavished on me, you would have given me your very *eyes,* if I had needed them! Alas! what has become of this delight and gratitude? Now, because I tell you the truth, you seem to think I hate you!

"Your new friends court and flatter you. They want you to do the like to them. Not that I am jealous of your making other friends in my absence: only let the friendship be honorable and sincere.

"O my children, I am suffering a mother's pangs for you over again in my longing to see Christ formed in you! Would that I could be with you, and speak in some kinder tone! You perplex me, and I know not what to write."

To the Romans

We have now arrived at the close of Paul's third missionary journey and the culminating point in his career, for it was the time of his decisive conflict with the Judaizing faction, in the course of which he wrote the four great evangelical epistles, the last and greatest of which we are about to review. Each of these letters marks a battle fought by the apostle on behalf of gospel faith and freedom: the epistle to the Romans signalizes the crowning victory.

The struggle was not an outward conflict alone, nor was the apostle engaged, like modern apologists, in shielding an old creed from new assaults. It is a novel and strange doctrine that he has to vindicate, whose foundations lay, indeed, in the person and teaching of Jesus, but which the Master had left to His servants to build up. The Christian principle had to be unfolded in its manifold bearings on life and history; it must be applied to the needs of the Gentile world, adjusted both to the Old Testament revelation and to the conditions of the existing age, a time of moral dissolution and deep spiritual unrest. It must be made permanently secure against the fierce reaction that arose on the part of Judaism, so soon as the full scope and consequences of the gospel began to be realized, and that was destined, in other forms, to recur again and again in the future.

There was only one man equal to this crisis, capable of grasping in all its breadth the situation created by the legalistic controversy at the close of the first Christian generation. The elements of the problem lay within Paul's own experience. His individual history had, virtually, been a solution and settlement of the questions at issue. They were such as these: How does the Law of Moses stand related to the new gospel of faith in Christ? How are the admission of un-circumcised Gentiles to the church and the indelible Abrahamic covenant to be reconciled? How can that be the true doctrine of Christ which His chosen people, by an overwhelming majority, re-pudiate? What security is there for morals under a reign of grace? Nay, what becomes of God's own righteousness and who will any longer reverence His Law upon a system of free pardon and universal amnesty for sinners? With his Pharisaic training, with his strict and delicate conscience and his intense faith in the religion of Israel, Paul realized, even more than his opponents, the force and the difficulty of these questions, and we can see that it cost him, both before and during the controversy, a prolonged struggle and the most strenuous mental effort to arrive at the solution he has given us. We must not suppose that inspiration superseded study on the part of the teach-ers of Scripture, that the gifts of the Holy Spirit served as a con-trivance for saving labor. On the contrary, it was with severe toil and by the unsparing exertion of his spiritual and intellectual powers that Paul composed his great doctrinal epistles, and the Holy Spirit prompted, sustained, and crowned the travail of his human will and reason. "I labor," he says, as he writes one of his most difficult letters (Col. 1:29; 2:1), "striving according to His power, which mightily works within me. . . . For I want you to know how great a struggle I have on your behalf."

In the Roman epistle the painful tension of feeling which we have marked in the last two letters has almost disappeared. We have no longer the quick movement, the vehement and halting utterance, the iron logic that runs hot and molten with the fire of passion through the pages of Galatians. This epistle is deliberate, luminous, ripe, and full. It is the work of a man sure of himself and of the ground that he has won, who is able now to survey calmly the field of this perilous contest and to gather up for the church in its completed results the issue and fruit of the momentous crisis through which his mission has been passing.

Occasion of Romans

The latest previous indications of time and place given us by the epistles (cf. 2 Cor. 8:1 with 2 Cor. 13:1) left the apostle in Macedonia for the second time and on his way to Corinth. This city he has now reached, completing the program of his present journey, and bringing to its close one great chapter of his mission, "so that from Jerusalem and round about as far as Illyricum I have fully preached the gospel of Christ" (Rom. 15:19, 23). He is about to sail for Jerusalem, bearing the contributions gathered in Macedonia and Achaia for the church there, and has a strong presentiment of peril waiting him in Judea (Rom. 15:25–27, 30, 31). For the future his thoughts are centered upon Rome. "For many years" he has longed to carry the gospel there, and when his visit to Jerusalem is once accomplished, the way will at last be clear for this project. Nor does he intend to halt at Rome; it will serve him for a stepping-stone to Spain (Rom. 1:10–15; Rom. 15:22–24, 28).

From the references of this epistle we conclude that Paul has carried out the plan previously announced, and now finds himself at Corinth, towards the end of the winter of A.D. 56–57, and preparing with the spring to journey again to Palestine. This inference is confirmed by Acts. In Acts 20:2, 3 we are told that "when he [Paul] had gone through those districts [an expression designed, perhaps, to include Illyricum along with Macedonia], and had given to them much exhortation, he came to Greece." There "he spent three months." A "plot was formed against him by the Jews" that compelled him to journey from Corinth by land, instead of crossing the Aegean, and by the Passover he had arrived at Philippi (Acts 20:6). From Macedonia he hastened on to reach Jerusalem before the Pentecost (Acts 20:16). The allusion in Romans 16:1 to "Phoebe, who is a servant of the church which is at *Cenchrea*" (the eastern port of Corinth), and in Romans 16:23 to "Gaius, host to me and to the whole church" (cf. 1 Cor. 1:14), also point to the apostle's residence at Corinth.

The gospel has now been planted in a line of great cities reaching from Jerusalem westward to the Ionian Sea. Ephesus, with the rich and populous province of Asia, had occupied Paul for nearly three years past, and a powerful Christianity was established there, through which the societies already existing to the east and west of it could join hands. Troas added a last link, to complete the chain of Pauline churches running unbroken from Antioch to Corinth. The revolt against Paul's authority and the reaction from his doctrine, for a time so threatening, seem to have subsided. The second letter to Corinth completed the work of the first in bringing that restless church to reason and order. The apostle addresses himself to the Romans with an ease of mind, a satisfaction in the conquests already gained and an eager and hopeful outlook into the future, in striking contrast to the tone in which he had written to Corinth and Galatia a few months before, and which go to show that the winter sojourn at Corinth was a time of peace and of reassurance to him. The Judaizers have now done their worst. The Gentile churches have rallied to Paul's side. The storm has spent itself and Paul's sky is clear again, inviting him to new and bolder adventure.

Rome now rises before the apostle's view. That mighty city, mistress of the world, center and crown of heathen civilization, must be the next object of his attack. Indeed, his eye had long been fixed upon Rome as the goal of his mission to the heathen. This commanding position once seized, the way would be open for advance to the regions beyond, until "as the lightning comes from the east, and flashes even to the west" (Matt. 24:27) the message of Christ carried by Paul should have reached the farthest limits of the Gentile world.

At this juncture, midway in his career and turning his face to a new world, the apostle feels it incumbent upon him to deliver a formal manifesto. He will give to the church a full and systematic account of the gospel that he preaches, in view especially of the vital questions raised and debated in the Judaistic controversy. What could be more timely than to write such an exposition of his teaching as this by way of introducing himself to the Christians of Rome? Within a few months he expects to find himself among them, and it was most important for the future progress of his work that he should win their support (Rom. 1:12; 15:24). He had already a number of friends, including two kinsmen, among the believers in Rome (assuming that Rom. 16:1–16 was addressed to the church there). Paul may well have hoped to make Rome for the west what Antioch had been for the east, a mother city for Gentile Christianity, a new center and headquarters for its missionary movements. Besides, he felt that the Roman church belonged, in an especial sense, to his charge as Gentile apostle (Rom. 1:10–15; 15:15, 16); that it was his duty, so soon as possible, to carry his gospel to the metropolis of paganism.

Such an epistle, while it paved the way for his approaching visit, would at the same time fore-arm this church against the Judaizing agitators, who in all likelihood would soon make their appearance at Rome, especially if they heard of Paul's intention to establish himself there.

Add to this, that in writing to the obscure Christian community at Rome Paul feels that he is in some sort addressing the imperial city itself. He writes as one who speaks *urbi et orbi*. There rises before his mind the image of the Roman city and Empire, which represented on one hand all the majesty of secular power and civil rule, and on the other all the shame and misery of Gentile sin.

The above considerations may serve as a suggestion of the views with which this letter was composed.

The Roman Church

The character and constituency of the church of Rome have been much discussed. There are two opposite views held on the subject, both deriving their support from the epistle. Plainly it was a *mixed church*, containing both Jewish and Gentile adherents (see Rom. 2:17; 11:13, etc.). But in what proportion were these elements mingled, and what was the attitude of the Roman church towards the great controversy of the hour? Those who assert its Gentile complexion have in their favor the express language of Romans 1:5, 6; 11:17–24. The opposite opinion is based on the general tenor of the epistle, on the fact that its arguments are directed throughout against Judaistic objections, on the prominence given to the problem of the destiny of Israel (Rom. 9—11), and on the specific appeal made to the Jewish conscience in Romans 2.

The critics who argue for the Jewish character of the church of Rome seem, however, to overlook the fact that the earliest Gentile converts had been in very many instances proselytes to Judaism and had received the gospel through Israelitish channels; of necessity, therefore, they took a lively interest in the Jewish question, and the difficulties arising from the relation of Christianity to the old religion pressed upon their minds only less severely than upon the Jewish

Christians themselves. On the whole, it appears to us most probable that the early Roman church contained a majority of Gentile Christians, but included a considerable number of men of the circumcision, who occupied an influential position in its ranks. Had the Jewish element been dominant among the Christian believers at Rome, had the Roman church been, in fact, the offspring of Jerusalem, it is difficult to see how Paul could have claimed it as falling within his own province.

From the silence of the epistle we gather that this community was not founded or directed by any single leader, whether apostle or apostolic man. The church having now existed for nearly thirty years and being established in most of the eastern cities of the Empire, a Christian society would inevitably form itself at Rome, for immigrants poured into the metropolis from all the provinces, as into London now, and every sect and school of thought found itself represented there. Among the multitude "from every nation under heaven" who formed Peter's congregation on the day of Pentecost, were "visitors from Rome, both Jews and proselytes" (Acts 2:10, 11). Some of these, we may suppose, were numbered among the three thousand converts of that day, and they would supply already the nucleus of a mixed Judeo-Gentile church. To these earliest Roman believers "Andronicus and Junias, my [Paul's] kinsmen" may have belonged, "who," he says, "were in Christ before me"; they had themselves done notable work as messengers of Christ, "who are outstanding," he adds, "among the apostles" (Rom. 16:7). In addition to those whom this first circle of Pentecostal disciples gathered round them in Rome, the church would be constantly gaining accessions by the migration to the capital of families and individual men converted to Christ in other places. Many of these, in all probability, came from churches owning the authority of Paul; some of them were the fruit of his own ministry. Hence the apostle could already, it appears, count quite a number of personal acquaintances among the brethren in Rome. The names he mentions (Rom. 16:1–16), if belonging to Rome, indicate that the church was of mixed origin, Greek in its constituency rather than Latin, and of catholic and cosmopolitan affinities. The population of Rome was at this time largely of Greek or Asiatic birth. "The Orontes," as Juvenal complains, "had flowed into the Tiber."

Like the rest of the epistles, this was written in Greek, and the language of the Roman church continued to be Greek both in its worship and literature until the end of the second century.

The church at Rome, therefore, stood in an independent and yet sympathetic and respectful attitude towards the apostle Paul. This we gather from the tone of the letter, and it accords with the probabilities of the case. There is nothing to show that any hostility to his person or teaching as yet existed here. At the same time, it is likely that the Judaistic tendency was present in a latent form here as elsewhere; afterwards it became pronounced and bitter, and alienated the Jewish Christians from Paul at the time when he most needed their sympathy (Phil. 1:15–17; Col. 4:11; 2 Tim. 4:16). At present, however, this church, while evangelical in its principles and in accord with the Pauline doctrines so far as it understood them, was probably defective in its theological knowledge, and not sufficiently aware of the danger threatening it from legalism nor alive to the gravity of the crisis through which Christianity was passing. The only view indicated in the letter which approaches heterodoxy, is that of the "weak" referred to in Romans 14, who held ascetic notions respecting food that caused dissension between them and their brethren. Their principles were of an Essenic rather than a Pharisaic type, and resembled the more developed asceticism inculcated shortly afterwards by the false teacher of Colossae (Col. 2:16–23).

In passing from Galatians to Romans, one is impressed by the conciliatory spirit in which the writer deals with Judaism. While vindicating more thoroughly than ever his universal gospel, Paul is wishful to disarm the prejudices of Jewish Christians and to meet all just objections on their part. In taking this course, he is only following the dictates of his own heart and tracing out the way in which his own birth and calling had been reconciled, in which the Gentile apostle and the ardent Jewish patriot within him had come to an understanding. This change of tone is due, we presume, to the absence of aggression on the part of Jewish Christians at Rome, as well as to the abating of the contest in Corinth and the appeasement of the storm within the apostle's own breast.

Threefold Conclusion of the Epistle

The letter, while written expressly for the church of Rome, is of so general a character that it may well have been utilized for the benefit of other churches at the same time. It would be felt that this exposition of the apostle's doctrine, so full and so timely, ought to be widely circulated. The alteration of a few words in Romans 1, the omission of a paragraph or two in Romans 15, with salutations and benediction adapted to each case, would make the epistle serve for other readers. The combining afterwards of three of these various endings may explain the threefold conclusion of the epistle (Rom. 15:33; 16:20, 27), which has always been a stumbling-block. On this theory, it is conjectured by some good scholars that the list of greetings contained in Romans 16:1–16 was addressed in reality *not to Rome*, but to some other place, most probably *to Ephesus, for* "Prisca and Aquila" were last heard of there (Rom. 16:3; cf. Acts 18:19), and there we meet with them again, in 2 Timothy 4:19; "Epaenetus," moreover, is greeted as "the firsr convert to Christ *from Asia*" (Rom. 16:5); add to this, that "Phoebe," the bearer of the letter, is introduced as "servant of the church which is at Cenchrea." Now, Cenchrea was the eastern port of Corinth, the port of departure for *Ephesus* (Acts 18:18, 19), but its name can scarcely have had the same interest for the Romans. At Ephesus Paul had spent a great part of three years, and there he had a multitude of friends. There is, however, as we have seen, no real difficulty in supposing these numerous and detailed greetings addressed to Rome, and the apostle wished to strengthen every link which bound him to his brethren in the imperial city.

Analysis of Romans

This is Paul's *magnum opus*. Here we see him at his greatest as a constructive thinker and theologian. The epistle to the Romans is the complete and mature expression of the apostle's main doctrines, which it unfolds in due order and proportion and combines into an organic whole. No other New Testament writing, except the epistle to the Hebrews, approaches so nearly the character of a doctrinal treatise. For the purposes of systematic theology, it is the most important book in the Bible. More than any other it has determined the course of Christian thought in its most fruitful epochs; its texts and definitions have been the battleground of momentous conflicts in the history of the church.

This epistle follows the internal development of its own thought, unaffected by local circumstances or associations of personal feeling. Here, again, it stands in signal contrast with the companion letters of its group. Its analysis is, therefore, comparatively easy, and at the same time of great importance. *The doctrinal argument* of the epistle forms its main body, extending from Romans 1:16—11:36. This is followed by a *hortatory* section (Rom. 12:1—15:13). *Personal matter* is confined to the Introduction (Rom. 1:1–15) and Conclusion (Rom. 15:14—16:27).

The INTRODUCTION consists:

(1) Of an elaborate and formal *greeting* (Rom. 1:1–7), containing an epitome of the *gospel* (Rom. 1:1–4) and an announcement of the writer's *apostleship* (Rom. 1:5, 6);

(2) A *statement of his feelings toward the Roman church* (Rom. 1:8–15)— his thankfulness for their widely known faith, his constant prayers for them, his wishes and endeavors to see them, and the debt he owes to them as being the apostle of the Gentiles.

The DOCTRINE of the epistle concerns two topics, principal and subordinate to each other: (A) that of *the salvation of Jews and Gentiles alike through faith in Jesus Christ* (Rom. 1:16—8:39), which is formally enunciated in Romans 1:16, 17, and (B) that of the *rejection of the Jewish nation as the people of God* (Rom. 9—11).

A. THE GOSPEL OF THE COMMON SALVATION, OR THE REVELATION OF THE DIVINE RIGHTEOUSNESS OF FAITH.

The treatment of this chief topic presents several well-marked sections, treating:

§ 1. Of *the guilty condition of mankind,* Romans 1:18—3:20:

(a) Notorious in the case of *the Gentiles,* whose idolatry by God's just judgment had borne fruit in abominable vice (Rom. 1:18–32);

(b) Concealed and excused, but no less real and still more culpable in *the Jews* (Rom. 2:1—3:8);

(c) *The universal indictment* being summed up in words of Scripture (Rom. 3:9–20).

§ 2. *God's method of making men righteous*, Romans 3:21—5:21:

(a) By a free gift of pardon, on condition of faith, grounded on Christ's redemptive sacrifice, and in harmony with God's personal righteousness, this being the ground of the provisional forgiveness attained under the Law, that is, in a word, *by justification* (Rom. 3:21–31);

(b) This method illustrated and defended by *the case of Abraham*, father of believers, whose was a righteousness of faith resting not on his own performances but on the supernatural power of God, certified to him by the word of promise, which looked on to Christ (Rom. 4);

(c) This method vindicated by its *experimental effects* (Rom. 5:1–11);

(d) The method traced to its *origin and creative ground*, as it derives our salvation from Christ, the spiritual head of the race, in a manner parallel to and countervailing that in which our sin and death flow from Adam, the natural progenitor (Rom. 5:12–21).

§ 3. *The Christian righteousness our death to sin*, or *Justification involving Sanctification*, Romans 6, 7. This is argued first *positively*, and that in two ways:

(a) As matter of principle, on the ground that faith unites the believer with Christ not in His death alone, but in *His resurrection and heavenly life*, its necessary sequel, a double truth symbolized by baptism (Rom. 6:1–14), and

(b) As a matter of fact and experience, since the Christian in becoming such committed himself by his own act to *God's holy service*, with its fruit in life eternal (Rom. 6:15–23).

The same consequence is established *negatively*; it is shown that there is no other way of holiness, for

(c) This is "what the Law could not do" (Rom. 8:3) since *under Law our nature gave birth to nothing but sin*, till in Christ's death this union was dissolved and we were wedded to the risen, life-giving Lord (Rom. 7:1–6);

(d) This, finally, Paul illustrates by his own experience, showing by his moral history, from childhood upwards, how *a better knowledge of the Law only led to a more hopeless enslavement to sin*, till he was rescued by Jesus Christ (Rom. 7:7–25).

§ 4. *The Christian righteousness the redemption of our whole nature*, Romans 8:

(a) It brings present *salvation from the guilt of sin* (Rom. 8:1–4), and *from its power over the mind* (Rom. 8:5–9) and even *over the body* (Rom. 8:10–13);

(b) It makes us *sons and heirs of God*, in fellowship with Christ (Rom. 8:14–17);

(c) It assures us of a *future glory*, in which along with our redeemed body the material creation will participate (Rom. 8:18–25);

(d) It supplies effectual help in prayer, confidence in all events, and the certainty that *the universe of God conspires to bless us* as the objects of His love in Christ (Rom. 8:26–39).

(e) Through this entire chain of blessings runs *the bestowment of the Holy Spirit*, which gives them their unity and their reality to our consciousness.

B. THE REPROBATION OF THE JEWISH PEOPLE

This second topic rose immediately out of the first. For if the gospel just expounded is "the power of God for salvation" and "to the Jew first," how is it that the Jewish people, who should be the best judges of its value, are everywhere rejecting it, and that many even of those who accept it differ radically from Paul in their views of its nature and are, as he maintains, virtually drawing back from it? For the apostle this was a most distressing problem, wounding to his heart while it threw continual and mortifying hindrances in the way of his mission. So important was the question of the attitude of Judaism toward the gospel that some excellent interpreters think that it formed in reality the motive of the whole epistle, and that the treatment of the former theme was designed mainly to lead up to this. Certainly, the writer has the second topic in view throughout the previous chapters.

God promised salvation to His people at the Messiah's coming. That Messiah has come, and yet they are rejecting Him to their own ruin! "Either, then, those promises or your gospel is false!" Such was the dilemma in which the apostle was placed by his opponents (note his counter-assertion in Rom. 15:8). Its fallacy lies, as he is quick to show, in the ambiguity of the essential middle term, *the people of God*. They are not the hereditary Jewish nation, but God's elect in every age, the men of faith. This he proves from the Old Testament, and so wrests from their hands his enemies' logical weapon and turns its keen edge upon themselves.

Expressing first his intense sorrow for his fellow-countrymen, who are refusing the gospel despite their glorious privileges, he affirms that, notwithstanding, _God's word has not failed_ (Rom. 9:6). This is the thesis of Romans 9—11, just as Romans 1:16, 17 is of Romans 1—8.

§ 1. _God's word has not failed_, for He is acting as He has ever done, _in the right of His own free and sovereign election_, whether in favor or punishment, uncontrolled by natural claims and human wishes,[1] Romans 9:6–29. The apostle's purpose here is not to disprove man's freedom and self-determination, but _to defend God's freedom_ as Ruler of men against Jewish dictation.

§ 2. _God's word has not failed, but Israel rejects His method of salvation by faith_, preferring to work out its own righteousness rather than to receive that which God offers, Romans 9:30—10:21.

§ 3. _God's word has not failed, for Israel will yet be saved_, Romans 11. Its present rejection of the gospel promotes the conversion of the Gentiles, from whom it will finally come back to Israel, when the program of the world's salvation will be completed.

So the apostle makes the objection disposed of under his second thesis serve to carry forward the argument of the first to its climax. Romans 11 crowns the description of the salvation of the individual in Romans 8, by the representation given in its concluding verses of _the final salvation of the world_. His theodicy terminates in a rapturous doxology (Rom. 11:33–36): "Oh, the depth of the riches both of the wisdom and knowledge of God!"

THE EXHORTATION

The practical part of the epistle may be very briefly summarized, Romans 12:1—15:13:

---

1. Observe that "the willer and the runner" of Romans 9:15, 16 (quoted from Ex. 33:19, where the entire context must be taken into account) is Moses, willing and running on behalf of the sinful people. "For He says to Moses, I WILL HAVE MERCY ON WHOM I HAVE MERCY," and so forth. So Paul was now "willing and running" with all his might to save his Israelitish brethren, and yet he knew that he had failed! God yields His prerogative to no man. To the prayer of Moses He allows much, but even Moses cannot force the Almighty's hand, nor dictate an act of mercy to another contrary to the divine will and judgment. Neither here nor anywhere is it hinted that the sinner, for himself, willing and running to seek mercy, may yet miss it! _God forbid!_ the apostle would have cried, had he heard of any so reading his words. Has he not said in the very next chapter (Rom. 10:13), "WHOEVER WILL CALL ON THE NAME OF THE LORD WILL BE SAVED"?

§ 1. It dwells in general terms:

> (a) *On consecration to God* (Rom. 12:1, 2),
>
> (b) *Sober estimation of oneself* (Rom. 12:3–8), and
>
> (c) *Brotherly conduct toward others* (Rom. 12:9–21).
>
> (d) *On civil obedience* (Rom. 13:1–7), and
>
> (e) *Neighborly duty* (Rom. 13:8–10), and
>
> (f) *Christian watchfulness* (Rom. 13:11–14).

§ 2. More specifically the apostle deals with the question of *doubtful meats* and the disputes connected with it, Romans 14:1—15:13. He enjoins on his readers:

> (a) *Mutual respect for each other's convictions*, especially in view of our responsibility to God (Rom. 14:1–12),
>
> (b) *The subordination of all such matters to the spiritual interests of the kingdom of Christ* (Rom. 14:13–23), and
>
> (c) *Devotion to the unity of the church*, after Christ's example (Rom. 15:1–12).

This is followed by a prayer for *joy and peace* in believing (Rom. 15:13).

The CONCLUSION consists:

(1) Of *an apology* for writing to the Romans, 15:14–21;

(2) An account of *Paul's position and intentions*, Romans 15:22–32;

(3) A *benediction*, which seems the natural close of the letter, Romans 15:33.

We have already spoken of the POSTSCRIPT (Rom. 16), with its long and varied list of greetings, by far the longest in the Epistles, closed by a solemn warning and a second benediction (Rom. 16:17–20). Then comes another brief list of mutual greetings (Rom. 16:21–23), closed by a full doxology in the style of the third group of the Pauline letters, to which we shall next proceed (Rom. 16:24–27).

We will paraphrase the following passages:

Romans 3:21–31: "Now, however, we have disclosed to us a *righteousness of God* that rests on another basis than that of Law, though both law and prophets bear witness to it. It is a righteousness imparted through faith in Jesus Christ, imparted to all believers alike. To *all*, I say, for all had sinned, all have lost the approval of God. Man's justification is gratuitous: it is wrought by God's grace, and by means of the redemption that is in Christ Jesus. Him God set forth openly, a bleeding sacrifice, availing through faith to expiate our sin. Thus God manifests His righteousness. He has shown how He could pass by the transgressions of former times and deal in forbearance with the world, waiting for the full disclosure of that righteousness made in our day, when we see God both just Himself and the Justifier of him who believes in Jesus.

" 'Where, then,' you ask, 'is our Jewish boasting?' It is excluded. 'What law forbids it?' The law of *faith*, to be sure; not that of works. For our argument is that man is justified by faith, and that his works can never justify him. Do you think that God is a God of *Jews* only? Is He not the God of Gentiles too? Yes, if 'the LORD is one' (Deut. 6:4), and He will justify circumcised men by faith, and uncircumcised men through the same faith. 'We are abolishing law,' you say, 'by this principle of faith'? Not in the least: we rather establish it!"

Romans 5:12–21: "It was *one* man through whom sin entered the world, and death through sin. Thus death reached all men, as all in fact committed sin (Rom. 3:23). For there was sin in the world before (Moses') Law, and the imputation of sin shows that, in some sense, there was law all the while.[2] From Adam down to Moses death reigned as king, even over men that had not sinned as Adam did, in transgression against revealed law. Now, Adam is the type of the Coming One.

"But there is a difference between the trespass and the gift of grace. Through the trespass of that one, the many died. If so, then God's grace, with the gift that comes by the grace of the one man Jesus Christ, has overflowed in far greater degree to the many. Again, it was from the trespass of a single sinner that the judgment began which issued in our condemnation; the gift of grace brings men to justification out of many trespasses. Surely if one man's trespass established the reign of death, much more must those reign in life through that other one, Jesus Christ, who receive His abounding grace and gift of righteousness.

---

2. We must admit that this is not the ordinary interpretation of Romans 5:13. But see Romans 2:14; also Romans 8:2 (*the law of sin and death*), and 1 Corinthians 15:56, showing that in Paul's mind *law, sin, and death* are concomitants.

"We come, then, to this conclusion: that as one trespass was the means of bringing all men into condemnation, so one act of righteousness is the means of bringing all men to justification and life. Through the disobedience of one man the many were constituted sinners, so through the obedience of one the many will be constituted righteous. Law intervened by the way, in order to multiply the trespass, but where sin multiplied, grace even more abounded. So that, finally, as sin has reigned triumphing in death, in like manner grace is to reign by means of righteousness unto life eternal, through Jesus Christ our Lord."

Romans 9:14–24: "What are we then to say about such cases as that of Jacob and Esau? Is God unjust in making this election? Far be that from Him! Remember what He said to Moses: 'I will have mercy on whomsoever I have mercy, and will pity whomsoever I may pity.' Clearly the choice lies not with the willing and striving man, but with the mercy-showing God. Take Pharaoh's case, on the other hand: 'For this very purpose,' says God, 'I raised thee up to such a height, that I might manifest in thee My power and have My name proclaimed throughout the earth.' He shows mercy, you see, or He hardens, in each case *as He will.* [In other words, God's will is absolutely free. He can act upon His own judgment in dealing with human affairs. None may share, none can defy His prerogative.]"

" 'But if He is Almighty,' someone asks, 'what right has He to find fault with His creatures?' What right have you, I reply, a mere man, to debate with God? How shall the creature say to its Creator, Why hast Thou thus made me? The potter surely is master of his clay! It is his to choose which part of the lump shall be made into a fine and which into a baser vessel. The case may be that God, though resolved to make an example of His displeasure and His sovereign power, has with great longsuffering borne with *vessels of wrath,* fit for nothing but destruction; purposing at the same time to make known the riches of His glory in *vessels of mercy,* that He had prepared for this end, I mean ourselves, whom He called into His kingdom from the ranks of the Gentiles as well as the Jews."

Transition to the
Third Group

Address at Miletus

Early in the year A.D. 57, Paul had finished his letter to the Romans and thus concluded one great epoch of his life and work. He now set his face to go up to Jerusalem. As we have already seen (Rom. 15:30–32), he looked forward to this visit with grave apprehensions. As he journeyed through Macedonia and along the coasts of Asia Minor and Syria, the shadows deepened across his path. "Bound in spirit," he says to the Ephesian elders, "I am on my way to Jerusalem, not knowing what will happen to me there except that the Holy Spirit solemnly testifies to me in every city, saying that bonds and afflictions await me" (Acts 20:22, 23; cf. Acts 21:4, 10–14). But he had not the least thought of turning from his course. And as the brethren at one place and another fling their arms about him to hold him back, he cries, "What are you doing, weeping and breaking my heart? For I am ready not only to be bound, but even to die at Jerusalem for the name of the Lord Jesus." His voyage was a series of farewells, that grew more and more affecting as he approached the Jewish capital. This journey of Paul's reminds us of nothing so much as of our Lord's last journey to Jerusalem. Was the apostle, like his Master, about to accomplish his decease at this fatal city, the murderess of her prophets? Was his sun now to set, at its high noon?

The address delivered at Miletus is, in effect, a valedictory charge (Acts 20:17–35). Paul is bidding good-bye to those whom he had set in charge of the great church of Ephesus, the fruit of his three years' labor there. "You," he says, "will see my face no more" (Acts 20:25), and it is a needless inference from 1 Timothy 1:3 to suppose that he did afterwards revisit this city. Five long years were to pass before any of his Gentile churches would see again the face of their beloved father in Christ. From this standpoint, anticipating the termination of his ministry, Paul reviews the past. He describes "the ministry which [he] received from the Lord Jesus" under three expressions which define admirably the principles and method of his teaching: he "went about preaching [heralding] *the kingdom*" (Acts 20:25; cf. 1 and 2 Thess.); he "testif[ied] solemnly of *the gospel* of the grace of God" (Acts 20:24; cf. Rom.—Gal.), and in the unfolding and enforcement of this message he "did not shrink from declaring to you *the whole purpose* of God," and "anything that was profitable" (Acts 20:20, 27), recall the rich practical and moral inferences drawn from the Pauline gospel especially in Corinthians.

But along with these reminders and this touching review of the past, there are words of warning that throw a piercing glance into the future. If Paul "not knowing what [would] happen to him there [in Jerusalem]," he foresaw the struggle that awaited in his absence the Asian churches: "I know that after my departure savage wolves will come in among you, not sparing the flock; and from among your own selves men will arise, speaking perverse things, to draw away the disciples after them" (Acts 20:29, 30). He seems to say, like Jesus to the Twelve, "*One of you* shall betray me!" This is a clear prediction of the rise of heresy within the Gentile church. The errors which Paul previously opposed were of a reactionary character, and arose almost inevitably from the connection of Christianity with Judaism and in the process of transition from the old faith to the new. But now we descry the approach of a storm from another quarter. A new conflict is impending; a ferment is beginning to work generated by the progress of the gospel, and that will arise out of the bosom of the church. The doctrine of Christ will itself be poisoned and perverted, and wolves will harry the flock under the guise of shepherds. These forebodings were realized in the course of a few years by the appearance of the Colossian heresy in the neighborhood of Ephesus, and by the further advance of the same type of error indicated in the Pastoral letters.

Paul's instructions to the elders of Ephesus not only point out the danger lying in the church's path, they indicate the means by which it is to be combated, the very means by which we shall find the apostle himself counter-working this evil in the epistles that now await our review. "Be on guard for yourselves," he says, "and for all the flock, among which the Holy Spirit has made you overseers [or bishops], to shepherd the church of God which He purchased with His own[1] blood. . . . I commend you to God and to the word of His grace, which is able to build you up and to give you the inheritance among all those who are sanctified" (Acts 20:28, 32). These words are full of significance. They mark the point at which the apostle's ministry assumes a mainly pastoral, instead of a mainly evangelistic character and aim. His work becomes conservative rather than aggressive. The care of the church is from this time his chief and absorbing concern. The letter to the Ephesians, the most labored and complete of his later epistles, is written for the "building up of the body of Christ." His thoughts are centered on the conception of the Christian community, in its relations to Christ and to God, to the counsels of eternity and the angelic powers, in its influence upon individual character and outward life, and on the realization of man's collective destiny which is to be accomplished by its means. Paul's ideal of the church rises to its lofty and grand proportions under the low roof of his prison-lodging at Rome. In the building of the church, in the consciousness of her corporate life, in the development of her organization, in her increased intelligence and moral strength, in her fuller sense of union with Christ and her more complete possession by His Spirit, lies the hope of her salvation amid the fierce conflicts and dissensions that will shortly burst forth around her.

Side by side with this expansion of the apostle's doctrine of the church, his teaching on the Person of Christ is correspondingly deepened and enriched, for these two truths are complementary and wedded to each other. Colossians and Ephesians, the two doctrinal epistles of this group, speak throughout "with reference to *Christ and the church*" (Eph. 5:32). This is their "mystery," the burden

---

1. "His own Son's blood" is Hort's tempting emendation.

of their revelation, even as *Christ and the cross* was the mystery of the last group of the epistles.

The Situation of the Apostle

The four writings which we have now to consider, Colossians, Philemon, Ephesians, Philippians, are *prison-letters*. You hear in each of them the clank of the chain upon the writer's arm. He is suffering for the cause of Gentile Christianity, and he glories in it (Eph. 3:1, 13; Col. 1:24). His arrest and long imprisonment, to all appearance so calamitous, "have turned out for the greater progress of the gospel" (Phil. 1:12). In Caesarea his confinement was somewhat close, and only private friends were allowed access to him (Acts 24:23), but at Rome, where he remained awaiting his trial for two years, the apostle was kept in what was called "free custody," being allowed to live under guard, chained by one wrist to a soldier, in his own hired house, and to preach and converse freely with all who came to him (Acts 28:30, 31). In this way he carried on an effective ministry, his position as a military prisoner bringing him into contact with many in the camp and the imperial household whom he could not otherwise have reached (Phil. 1:13). He had become an object of public interest and sympathy in Rome, pleading for Christ as an "ambassador in chains" (Eph. 6:19, 20). His arrival at the city and the courage and energy which he showed under these adverse circumstances proved a great stimulus to the Roman church, and led on all hands to a more vigorous prosecution of the work of Christ.

There were "some, to be sure," animated by Judaistic feeling (cf. Phil. 1:15, 17 with Col. 4:11), whose zeal was due to "envy and strife," who did their utmost to oppose Paul's influence and aggravate his trials, but even in their activity he rejoiced, for it helped to diffuse the knowledge of Christ. With all its drawbacks, Paul's situation at Rome (A.D. 60–62) brought considerable advantages with it. He endured its privations with the utmost cheerfulness. Never had his experience been so joyous or his confidence in the cause of Christ so high as when he wrote to the Colossians (Col. 1:6) and Philippians (Phil. 1:19, 20), towards the end of this captivity; never had he been so sensibly assured that all things were working together for good, both for himself and for the kingdom of God.

What we thus learn as to Paul's relations to the church of Rome held good in regard to the church at large. The apostle had become, in the most public manner possible, a martyr for Christ. His attempted murder in Jerusalem, his trial before the Sanhedrin and at the Procurator's court, his appeal to Caesar, his perilous voyage and long detention in Rome, all this train of events fixed the attention and admiration of his fellow-believers upon him. It was felt that Paul, more than any other man, was the champion and representative before the world of the Christian faith, "set for defense of the gospel." Everywhere the keenest sympathy was evoked by the story of his sufferings. Only the most fanatical Judaists were disposed any longer to question his apostolic claims. "The signs of a true apostle," as he had pathetically written to the Corinthians (2 Cor. 11:23; 12:11, 12), were "performed" in him, "with all perseverance" as well as "by signs and wonders and miracles." Who could deny that he was "in far more labors, in far more imprisonments, beaten times without number, often in danger of death"? Paul's personal position, his place in the love and reverence of the church, was now secure. He needs no longer to waste a word upon his own defense. We mark in the letters of this period a calm sense of authority, a consciousness, blended with the deepest humility, of the unique grandeur of his office and his unquestioned place among the chief apostles, such as we scarcely find in earlier epistles, or only in its first traces in the letter to the Romans (Rom. 1:5; 11:13; 15:15–17). It was in the capacity of Nero's prisoner at Rome, Christ's bondsman for the Gentiles, that Paul rose to the full unassailable height of his sublime mission. He now visibly becomes what he has ever since remained in the eyes of the universal church, as *the apostle*.

Along with this advancement in outward influence, Paul's spiritual life had grown more calm and deep. The epistle to the Philippians takes us into the sanctuary of his inward experience. The trials of recent years have brought their blessing to himself. His life had many times hung in the balance. His condition as a prisoner was irksome in the extreme, to a man of his temperament, and in earlier days his high spirit and active disposition would have chafed against it exceedingly. He has been thrown in upon himself, with leisure for meditation such as he had never enjoyed since the "three years" spent in Arabia. During all this time of suspense, of solitude, and hardship to flesh and blood, Christ has been his companion, Christ his continual study. The apostle's one aim has been to "know Him, and the power of His resurrection, and the fellowship of His sufferings, being conformed to His death" (Phil. 3:10). The cross of Christ which had given him his message of salvation to the world, supplied also his model and personal ideal (Phil. 3:10). He was filling up the part assigned him in the fellowship of Christ's afflictions (Col. 1:24). Such thoughts had brought him not comfort alone, but a strange and overflowing delight. He was "strengthened with all power, according to His glorious might, for the attaining of all steadfastness and patience; joyously." From the emperor downward, there was no man in Rome so happy as the prisoner Paul. Of "fears within" we hear no more, and "conflicts without" do not vex him as they did (2 Cor. 7:5). Death and life are equal to him; in every state he is content (Phil. 1:20–24; 4:11–13). Living in the undimmed light of Christ's fellowship and in the love and confidence of Christ's people throughout the world, nothing can make him sorrowful, and he writes to the Philippians, "I rejoice and share my joy with you all" (Phil. 2:17). In Paul's soul it was summertime. His prison lodging stood next-door to paradise.

Meyer, and some other interpreters, have maintained that the three Asian letters (Eph., Col., Phile.) were written *from Caesarea* (A.D. 57–59), not from Rome. The positive grounds alleged for this are very slight. On the other hand, Ephesians and Colossians resemble Philippians and differ from the letters of the former group in so marked a way, that the later date and place of composition are more probable. It was at Rome, moreover, and not in the prison of Caesarea, that the apostle had the liberty of preaching implied in Ephesians 6:19, 20 and Colossians 4:3, 4. To Rome the runaway slave Onesimus is likely to have come. And surveying the Gentile world from Rome, Paul could fitly speak of the gospel as "*in all the world* . . . bearing fruit and increasing" (Col. 1:6).

The Colossian Heresy

One day there reached Paul's lodging at Rome a visitor from Asia, of the name of *Epaphras*. He was minister and founder of the church at Colossae, a Greco-Phrygian town in the province of Asia, situated, with its neighbor cities of Laodicea and Hierapolis, more than a hundred miles inland from Ephesus. So far the influence of Paul's ministry at the latter city had extended, although he had never himself visited this secluded region. Epaphras came to the apostle in great trouble. A teacher had appeared in his church (we say *a* teacher, for the denunciations of Col. 2:8, 16, 18 point to a single person) answering too truly to the apostle's description in Acts 20:29, 30, "speaking perverse things, to draw away the disciples after" him. This new teacher was a man of plausible style and large pretensions; at the same time, there was an air of humility about him and an ascetic rigor well calculated to influence in his favor undiscerning minds. In learning and argument Epaphras probably found himself overmatched, and he was in fear lest his flock should be shaken and divided in their faith, if not wholly led astray. Hence he comes with his report to Paul, who had sent him upon this charge to Colossae in the first instance (Col. 1:7, "a faithful servant of Christ *on our behalf*"), seeking advice and help. The apostle writes accordingly, and he intends, upon his release, to make it one of his first objects to visit Colossae and confront in person this new movement (Phile. 22).

Such was the occasion of the epistle to the Colossians. To understand its purport, we must endeavor to realize the nature of the teaching against which it was directed. This doctrine differed essentially from that of the Judaizers of Galatia and Corinth. While Jewish in outward guise (Col. 2:11, 14, 16), its inspiration was drawn from another source. The Colossian heresy bore the name of "philosophy" (Col. 2:8); it had, "the appearance of wisdom" (Col. 2:23) and appealed to men of intellectual tastes. Along with its Jewish dress and philosophical affinities, two main principles are conspicuous in its tenets, *reverence for the angelic powers* (see Col. 2:10, 15, 18), and *contempt for the body* (Col. 2:20–23).

Under these characteristics we can detect the first beginnings of the great Gnostical movement which culminated in the early part of the second century. We need not be surprised to find symptoms of this tendency in the infancy of the church. Gnosticism was already in the air; as B. Jowett says, it constituted "the mental atmosphere of the Greek cities of Asia, a conducting medium between heathenism and Christianity," a common solvent, one might rather say, of heathenism, Judaism, and Christianity. Judaism had been subject to its influence in the Greek cities of the East for two hundred years. The

Alexandrian "philosophy" embodied in the extensive works of Philo, Paul's contemporary, is nothing but a Jewish Gnosticism, an amalgam of Greek idealism and Oriental theosophy with the Mosaic system. Philo's whole endeavor was to put the new wine of Plato into the old bottles of Moses, and to persuade himself that this foreign infusion had been there from the first. If the Pharisees were the *High Church* of Judaism, then these philosophical Hellenists constituted its *Broad Church*. Now, it is from this quarter, the very opposite to that which gave rise to the legalistic movement, that the errors proceeded which the apostle has here to combat.

This system of thought had for its root-idea, in common with Eastern philosophy and theosophy in general, a belief in *the absolute separation of God from the world and the intrinsic evil of matter*. Hence it interposed, on the one hand, a hierarchy of "angels," or "powers," or "words"[2] (as they are designated by Philo), in order to mediate by manifold grades between God and the finite creation, and, on the other hand, a course of ritual and ascetic purifications by which man should rise above his bodily condition into communion with the spiritual world. The Jewish sect of the Essenes, who lived a hermit life in Palestine, and are supposed by many to have given an impulse to the teaching of John the Baptist, and even of Jesus, held similar views. To these principles the doctrines and vocabulary of Judaism were accommodated by the free use of allegory. The Colossian heresy was a first essay in the attempt to bring the gospel of Christ under the scope of this Gnostic philosophy of religion. A similar leaven was already at work in the Corinthian doubters of the resurrection, and in a milder form, perhaps, in the vegetarianism of the "weak brethren" of Rome. We trace its further development in the various errors and corruptions denounced by the Pastoral epistles, by the Apocalyptic letter to the seven churches of Asia, by the first epistle general of John, and indirectly by the fourth Gospel which has in view men who denied both the incarnation and the full divinity of Jesus Christ.

Naturally enough, this heresy sought in the first instance to graft itself upon the broad and innovating Pauline doctrine. The leaders of the movement may easily have claimed to be disciples of Paul and

---

2. Or *Mahatmas*, in the language of Hindu theosophists.

continuers of his work in the sphere of higher religious thought. In conflict with such opponents, the apostle's attitude becomes as much conservative as against the legalists it had been liberal and progressive, for he was dealing with men like those of whom John writes, "who *goes too far* and does not abide in the teaching of Christ" (2 John 9), claiming for this reason to be the "advanced thinkers" of the day. These men of progress and enlightenment showed themselves, after all, but narrow and illiberal sectarians. For the old Jewish exclusiveness of race they substituted a Gnostic exclusiveness of intellectual caste. They sought to form a church within the church, reserving the higher privileges of religion for those who were initiated into their esoteric "mysteries." Of this tendency we have clear indications in the language of Colossians 1:27—2:3, and possibly in Ephesians 1:8, 17, and so forth. There was in this first heresy a strange blending of elements of error afterwards divergent, a combination of rationalism with asceticism, of ceremonialism with mysticism. The personality of the heretical leader does not come clearly into view. His behavior was a mixture of self-aggrandizement and humility (Col. 2:8, 16, 18, 22), of affected spirituality joined with pettiness and earthliness of mind (Col. 2:18, 21, 23).

This new doctrine, under the pretense of developing Christian faith, tended to overthrow it from its foundations. For (1) it impeached *the sufficiency of Christ* as revealer of God and redeemer of men; (2) it endangered *the unity of the church* centering in Him, and dissolved the bonds of Christian fellowship; (3) it destroyed *the divine character of creation* and *the natural order of human life*. To these imperiled principles the Asian letters are devoted.

ADDITIONAL NOTE: In this group, rejected wholesale by F. C. Baur (see p. 41), the genuineness of *Philippians*, and of *Philemon*, is now admitted on all hands. *Colossians* is generally accepted as Pauline, with some misgiving as to interpolation in particular passages. The Tübingen School still contest *Ephesians*, for which Harnack, however, gives his weighty vote. On the authenticity of this last, see especially the article on *Epistle to the Ephesians* in Smith's *Dictionary of the Bible*, edition 2, also in Hastings' *Dictionary of the Bible*, and that in the *Encyclopedia Britannica*. Hort's *The Romans and the Ephesians*, and chapter 1 in the *Expositor's Bible* (*Eph.*), may also be serviceable. This question is bound up with that treated in the first section of the following chapter.

Connection of Colossians and Ephesians

These two letters are intimately allied in their contents and subject-matter. The relationship of the three Pastorals, or of Galatians and Romans, only approaches the closeness of the tie that binds in one Colossians and Ephesians. This parallelism is conspicuously manifest in the sections relating to family duties (Eph. 5:22—6:9; Col. 3:18—4:1), but it exists equally in many other passages, and those dealing with the chief subjects of the epistles: compare, *for example*, Ephesians 1:21–23 with Colossians 1:16–19, 2:10, 15; Ephesians 4:14–16 with Colossians 2:19; Ephesians 4:22–25 with Colossians 3:8–10; Ephesians 5:19, 20 with Colossians 3:16, 17. Both epistles are occupied with the thoughts of *the lordship of Christ*, and *the unity of His body the church* growing out of its relationship to Him, but in Colossians the emphasis falls upon the former, in Ephesians upon the latter of these truths. In both *the new moral life* of Christian believers is set forth at large, more adequately than in any previous epistle, and upon the same general lines, but the injunctions of Colossians start from the idea of the believer's union with Christ in His exalted heavenly life, those of Ephesians from that of the unity of the Spirit existing in the church on earth. In both the same strong desire is exhibited, appearing also in the prayer of Philippians 1:9, 10, for *a deeper Christian knowledge* in the church, such as would protect it from the

seductions of intellectual error and rob them of their force (see Eph.
1:17, 18; 4:13, 14; Col. 1:9; 2:2, 3; 3:10).

These epistles are pinned together by the identical references of
Ephesians 6:21, 22 and Colossians 4:7, 8. They were sent by the same
messenger, *Tychicus*, charged in each case with the same commission.
Tychicus had accompanied Paul to Jerusalem as a representative of the
Asian churches (Acts 20:4). He is found in the apostle's service
again, when some four years later he wrote the epistle to Titus (Titus
3:12). Bearing these priceless documents with many added verbal messages and greetings, Tychicus landed at Ephesus and thence traveled
inland to Colossae, visiting, doubtless, other churches on the way.

To the nearest of the intervening churches, that of *Laodicea*,
the Colossians are directed to communicate their own epistle, re-
ceiving at the same time for their perusal a letter of the apostle's to
be forwarded from Laodicea ("and you, for your part read my letter *that
is coming* from Laodicea," [Col. 4:16]). Archbishop Ussher suggested,
two hundred years ago, that this "letter from Laodicea" was none other
than *our epistle to the Ephesians*, and his hypothesis during later years
has found many supporters, including scholars so eminent as Bengel,
Lightfoot, Godet, Beet, A. Sabatier, Hort, and A. Robertson. The two
letters excellently serve to illustrate and complete each other.

Moreover, the characteristics of the longer epistle make it extremely difficult to suppose that it was designed for the church of Ephesus alone. Observe (1) *the very general terms* in which the letter is
couched. Not only are personal tidings and greetings wanting, which
Tychicus might have supplied by word of mouth, but there is an entire absence of those references to the condition of the particular
church addressed, to the circumstances of its origin and the apostle's
earlier associations with it, which Paul delights to make in writing to
old acquaintances. This is most surprising, when we remember that
he had lived at Ephesus longer than in any other city of his mission
(contrast the allusions of Acts 20:18–25), and it cannot be explained by any supposed change of manner, for we find him writing
in an almost familiar style to the Colossians, whom he knew only
through Epaphras and Philemon. (2) The language of Ephesians
1:15, 16 (cf. Col. 1:4; contrast Phil. 1:3–7), also of Ephesians 3:2; 4:21,
taken in its natural sense, signifies that the writer has in view some
readers of whose faith he *only knows by report;* he is not in all cases sure

of the extent and quality of their Christian knowledge. Can we conceive Paul writing thus of his Ephesian children in the faith? (3) There is *an official distance and normality* in the writer's attitude, such as we find in no other epistle, and very different from Paul's manner toward his friends and disciples. Not once does he address his readers as "brethren" or "beloved": "my brethren" in Ephesians 6:10 is an insertion of the copyists. There is not a single word of familiarity or endearment in the whole letter. The benediction at the end (Eph. 6:23, 24) is given in the third person, not in the second as everywhere else: "Peace be to *the brethren!* . . . Grace be with *all those who love* our Lord Jesus Christ"; not "Grace be *with you."* Nowhere do we see less of *this* or *that* church, and more of *the* church; nowhere less of the man, and more of the apostle in Paul.

Two facts of external evidence confirm this presumption. (4) *The absence of the words "in Ephesus"* in the address of the epistle as it appears in the Vatican and Sinaitic manuscripts, our oldest and best witnesses to the Greek text. Origen, who wrote early in the third century, Basil in the fourth, and Jerome in the fifth, testify that this reading of Ephesians 1:1 prevailed in the earliest times.[1] (5) Finally, it appears from Tertullian that Marcion, a heretical doctor of the second century, actually *entitled this epistle "To the Laodiceans"!* Nor does Tertullian appeal to the words of 1:1, as he would certainly have done if "in Ephesus" stood there in the accepted text of his time; he quotes the title of the epistle, and common tradition, against the heretic. It does not appear that this designation in any way furthered Marcion's peculiar views. At the same time, there is no evidence beyond that of Marcion for any *title* but the usual one. Other writers of the second century, including Irenaeus, Clement of Alexandria, and Origen himself (who seems to have known nothing of the reading "that are in Ephesus") quote the epistle as "to the Ephesians." The whole tradition of the early church associated it with Ephesus.

---

1. Supposing this reading to be genuine, we should probably translate: "To the saints, those that are indeed faithful in Christ Jesus" (Eph. 1:1). Compare the last words of the letter of Ephesians: "Grace be with all those who love our Lord Jesus Christ with a love incorruptible"; also Colossians 1:2.

The *circular hypothesis* of Ussher appears to reconcile these discordant facts, and to account for the peculiarities which we have
pointed out in the epistle and which have been strongly urged
against its authenticity. On this view, it was designed for Ephesus indeed, but at the same time for *a circle of Asian churches* (cf. John's
"seven churches that are in Asia"), including some, such as that of
Laodicea, which Paul had not been able to visit, whose members had
"not personally seen [his] face" (Col. 2:1) and about whose state he
was imperfectly informed. Tychicus may have been charged to read
the letter in the churches through which he passed, finally deposit-
ing the autograph in Ephesus, or a number of copies may have been
prepared at first for circulation from Ephesus, which was the most con-
venient center for western Asia Minor. Ephesus being the metropolis of the province and claiming a peculiar right in Paul, would
naturally regard the document as specially its own, and it would become known to churches in other quarters through Ephesus. Marcion,
who was a native of Asia Minor, has, it may be, preserved a genuine
fragment of local tradition testifying to the wider destination of the
letter. We venture, on the above grounds, to read this epistle as *the
general epistle of Paul the apostle to the churches of Asia.*

While in its contents and vocabulary Ephesians resembles Colossians very closely, in their style one feels a considerable difference.
Colossians is terse, vigorous, pointed, and sometimes highly ellipti-
cal and abrupt. Ephesians is the most diffuse and flowing of the
apostle's writings. Nowhere does Paul heap together so many syn-
onyms; nowhere else does he express his thoughts with such fullness
of phrase, or return so often to the same idea, as in Ephesians. In
Colossians, however, we have some notable passages marked by this
amplitude of style, which is a new feature in the apostle's manner as
a writer, due perhaps to the leisure of prison and the habit of meditation which it fostered (see Col. 1:9–11, 16–20, 27–29), but in
Ephesians this peculiarity is carried to its furthest extent, and marks
the entire course of the epistle.

This difference represents not, as some critics argue, a difference of authorship, but *a difference of mood* in the same author. The
letters are the outcome of two contrasted states of mind, such as al-
ternate rapidly in a mobile nature like Paul's. Galatians and Romans exhibit the same contrast, only to a lesser degree. Colossians is

a letter of discussion, Ephesians of reflection. In the former we behold Paul in spiritual conflict, in the latter his soul is at rest. Writing to the flock of Epaphras at Colossae, he is struggling with a new problem profound and far-reaching in its issues, in regard to which he is at a greater disadvantage inasmuch as it has come upon a distant church and one comparatively unknown to him (Col. 1:28—2:3). The Ephesian letter, on the other hand, is the most tranquil and meditative, the most calmly expansive and John-like, that Paul has ever composed; only here and there (Eph. 4:14; 6:10–20; cf. also footnote in ch. 10) does it remind us of the conflict through which he has passed and which he sees awaiting the church in the near future. The first is like the mountain stream cleaving its way with swift passage, by deep ravines and sudden, broken turnings, through some barrier thrown across its path; the second is the far-spreading lake in which its chafed waters find rest, mirroring in their clear depths the eternal heavens above.

Analysis of the Two Epistles

The relation of these two profound epistles to each other will be better understood, if we place them in our final analysis side by side. In the order of thought, and in virtue of its more definite aim, Colossians leads the way. Both letters consist of *doctrine and exhortation* in nearly equal proportions, the doctrine in Colossians taking a polemical, in Ephesians a devotional turn, while the exhortation in both epistles is richly ethical. In both, at about the same point, Paul weaves into his doctrinal exposition a statement *concerning himself*, relating to his Gentile apostleship and the imprisonment it has brought upon him: Colossians 1:23—2:5; Ephesians 3:1–13. The last section of Colossians (Col. 4:7–17) consists of *personal information and greetings* of the most interesting nature, such as, beyond the reference to Tychicus, are wholly wanting in the companion letter.

Introduction to Colossians, 1:1–14

This consists of SALUTATION (Col. 1:1, 2), THANKSGIVING (Col. 1:3–8), and PRAYER (Col. 1:9–14). (In the epistles of this group a prayer regularly follows the opening thanksgiving, a custom only anticipated in 1 and 2 Thess.)

The Christian hope is the center of the thanksgiving, with *the ministry of Epaphras* for its secondary topic. The need of *deeper knowledge* is the keynote of the prayer, to be attended with *thankfulness for the blessings of redemption*.

A. THE DOCTRINE OF COLOSSIANS, Colossians 1:15—2:23. This we may again divide into an *expository* Colossians 1:15—2:7, and *polemical* part, Colossians 2:8–23.

§ 1. Concerning *the Redeeming Son and His kingdom*, Colossians 1:15–20. He is the image of God, and the Lord and Head of all creation, Colossians 1:15. This great affirmation is applied:

(1) To *the natural universe*, where the basis of His kingdom lies deep and wide as the foundation of the world. "All things, [angels included,] have been created by Him and for Him, . . . and in Him all things hold together." In other words, Christ is the end, the mediating cause, and the uniting bond of the existing universe, Colossians 1:16, 17.

(2) To *the church*, the new creation (including "things . . . in the heavens"), over which in virtue of His cross and resurrection Christ holds a corresponding headship, Colossians 1:18–20. The work of Christ the Redeemer is thus based upon and made parallel to that of Christ the Creator.

§ 2. Concerning *the salvation of the readers*, Colossians 1:21–23.

This is briefly touched upon, with reference to their former sinful state (Col. 1:21); to the means and the purpose of their reconciliation to God (or *to Christ*: cf. Col. 1:22 with Col. 1:13; 2 Cor. 5:9, 10), and to the subjective conditions on which it depends (Col. 1:23).

§ 3. Concerning *the apostle and his mission*, Colossians 1:23—2:7:

(1) In *its general aspect*: his sufferings for the cause of the Gentiles (Col. 1:24), his great commission to reveal the mystery of their heritage in Christ (Col. 1:25–27), his faithful and laborious discharge of this office (Col. 1:28, 29).

(2) In *its particular relation to the readers*: his anxiety for those to whom he had been unable personally to minister, at this time of trial to their faith (Col. 1:1–4); his joy in their steadfastness (Col. 1:5), and appeal for its continuance (Col. 1:6, 7).

Having laid the foundation for his argument in the sovereignty of Christ, and put himself upon a proper footing with his readers, Paul now delivers his assault against the enemy at Colossae.

§ 4. Concerning *the new teacher and his philosophy*, Colossians 2:8–23:

(1) Which *robs Christ of His glory, and believers of their completeness in Him*, Colossians 2:9–15;

(2) Which carries them back to *superseded Jewish observances*, supplemented by an *angel-worship* derogatory to Christ's headship of the church, Colossians 2:16–19;

(3) Which imposes *arbitrary ascetic rules*, that hurt the body while they fail to mortify the flesh, Colossians 2:20–23.

B. THE ETHICS OF COLOSSIANS, Colossians 3:1–4.

Observe how the doctrine of the exalted Christ runs through these exhortations, glorifying and exalting all the moral relationships of life. The new life is set forth:

(1) In its *hidden union with Christ in heaven*, soon to be revealed on His appearing, Colossians 3:1–4.

(2) From this union is inferred (*a*) the believer's *separation from old sins* (Col. 3:5–9), (*b*) his *investment with the new Christ-like character*, distinguished by spiritual intelligence and the widest human charity (Col. 3:10, 11).

So much for the individual life of the Christian. His social life in the church is one

(3) Of *brotherly affection and forgiveness*, Colossians 3:12–14;

(4) Of *all-controlling peace*, Colossians 3:15;

(5) Of *mutual edification by word and song*, Colossians 3:16;

(6) Of *consecration to Christ and thankfulness to God in everything*, Colossians 3:17.

Peculiar to Colossians and Ephesians are the exhortations:

(7) To a right Christian discharge of *family duties*, those of husband and wife, parent and child, master and slave (Col. 3:18—4:1). The last of the three Paul dwells upon here, with an eye to the case of Onesimus and Philemon.

Finally, exhortations follow of a general character:

(8) To *constancy in prayer and thanksgiving*, prayer being asked especially for the apostle in his bonds, Colossians 4:2–4

(9) To *watchful behavior and wise speech among men of the world*, Colossians 4:5, 6.

Of the concluding personal section we have spoken already, Colossians 4:7–18.

Introduction to Ephesians, 1:1–19

After the SALUTATION (Eph. 1:1, 2), the apostle enters upon an ACT OF PRAISE, the most extended and sublime in his epistles (Eph. 1:3–14). This is followed by a PRAYER, less sustained indeed but of great fullness and weight, from which he proceeds to the doctrine of the letter without any perceptible break. The three first chapters are steeped in devotion: the apostle teaches, as it were, upon his knees.

The ACT OF PRAISE is divided by its threefold refrain, "to the praise of the glory of His grace . . . the praise of His glory," into three sections, or stanzas (Eph. 1:6, 12, 14), setting forth in succession *the eternal purpose of divine grace*, its *present communication to the believer*, and *the future glory* for which it seals both Jew and Gentile.

The PRAYER asks on the readers' behalf for enlightenment to know three things: *the hope to which God calls them*, *the wealth that He possess in them*, and *the surpassing greatness of His power toward them* measured by the resurrection of Christ (Eph. 1:18–21).

A. DOCTRINE OF EPHESIANS, Ephesians 1:20—3:13

The teaching of this letter, as we have seen, rises out of its opening prayer. Paul instructs his readers:

§ 1. Concerning *what God wrought in the Christ*, Ephesians 1:20–23,

raising Him from the dead, lifting Him above all angelic powers to the headship of the universe, and giving Him, thus enthroned, to the church for its Head; while it in turn is the body He inhabits in whom dwells the fullness of that divine power and glory which replenish the universe.

§ 2. Concerning *what God has wrought in the readers* through Christ, Ephesians 2. And this:

(1) In *their individual salvation* (Eph. 2:1–10), raising them from the death of sin and the bondage of Satan to life in the knowledge of God's love and the fellowship of the ascended Christ.

(2) In *their incorporation as Gentiles with the people of God*. Jews and Gentiles are reconciled to each other, as both are reconciled to God, by the cross, that they may be "built together into a dwelling of God in the Spirit" (Eph. 2:11–22). This is the most distinctive paragraph in the epistle, the fullest presentment we have of Paul's conception of the church.

§ 3. Concerning *what God wrought in the apostle toward this end*, Ephesians 3:1–13,

making through him, the unworthiest of men, a revelation of unspeakable glory, hidden in God's counsels from the beginning of the world, which the angels are watching with profound interest.

This brings the apostle to his knees again, and he concludes his doctrine with a renewed act of prayer and praise: of prayer for *power to comprehend this revelation* (Eph. 3:16–19), and of praise to Him who is able *in boundless measure to supply this power* (Eph. 3:20, 21). So the doctrine of the epistle ends as it began, in worship.

B. ETHICS OF EPHESIANS, Ephesians 4:1—6:20

This homily is an expansion of the corresponding address in Colossians, but is more discursive, and treats at length of several points barely indicated there. The apostle enjoins:

§ 1. *Union in the church,* based on the seven unities of its faith, Ephesians 4:1–6.

§ 2. *The use of the various gifts of individuals* to promote the growth of the body of Christ, Ephesians 4:7–16.

Ephesians 4:7–16 form the most remarkable homiletical section, as Ephesians 2:11–22 the distinctive doctrinal paragraph of the epistle. Here the apostle discusses: (1) *the source of the endowments of the Christian ministry,* which are the spoil of the triumphant Christ, and (2) *their use in organizing and training the church,* so that each member may do his part in building up God's temple.

§ 3. *Separation from old Gentile vices,* to be replaced by the corresponding *new Christian virtues,* Ephesians 4:17—5:14.

Falsehood, anger, theft, malice, impurity, covetousness, foolish talk are specified (Eph. 4:25—5:6). All is summed up in the contrast between the "children of light and darkness" (Eph. 5:7–14). Note how every moral rule is enforced by evangelical reasons.

§ 4. Brief exhortations follow, bearing on *social Christian life,* Ephesians 5:15–21:

To *practical wisdom, sobriety,* and *spiritual animation* finding vent in song and thanksgiving, and to *mutual subjection.*

§ 5. The three relations of *family life* occupy Ephesians 5:22—6:9.

The apostle dwells at length on *marriage,* setting forth under this idea once more the union of Christ and the church.

§ 6. The closing address scarcely comes under the title of ethics, Ephesians 6:10–20. It is the apostle's *call to arms!*

A severe conflict awaits the church (read "Finally" in Eph. 6:10: the adv. is that of Gal. 6:17), and Christ's soldiers must be equipped and forearmed to meet it (cf. Eph. 4:14).

The paragraph relating to Tychicus (Eph. 6:21, 22), and a short and quite unique BENEDICTION (Eph. 6:23, 24), conclude the letter.

The Epistle to Philemon

Along with Tychicus there journeyed to Colossae a certain *Onesimus*, whom Paul commends as "*our* faithful and beloved brother, who is one of your *number*" (Col. 4:9). The note addressed to Philemon, along with the letter to the Colossian church, explains about this Onesimus. He was a runaway slave of Philemon, whose steps had been providentially directed to Paul in his prison. The fugitive had been converted to the faith of Christ. He has proved himself a most lovable and serviceable man; the apostle is loath to part with him, calls him "my child whom I have begotten in my imprisonment . . . my very heart" (Phile. 10–12). But he has no right to keep Onesimus, and he sends him home to his master, "no longer as a slave, but more than a slave, a beloved brother" (Phile. 16).

With Philemon and his family the apostle was well acquainted (Phile. 1, 2). Philemon recognized Paul as his father in Christ (Phile. 19–21). We may imagine that, being a man of property, he had occasion to visit Ephesus, the capital of his province, and there had heard the gospel from Paul six or seven years ago. Philemon's son Archippus is mentioned in the epistle to the Colossians, in a way which suggests that he was at this time ministering to the church of Laodicea (Col. 4:16, 17; Phile. 2). Paul speaks of him, doubtless for this reason, as "my . . . fellow-soldier" (cf. Phil. 2:25; 2 Tim. 2:3).

This delightful little letter has a special value for several reasons:

(1) For the light which it throws on *the apostle's disposition in private life*, exhibiting the fine courtesy, the exquisite tact and even playfulness of wit, which were not the least precious traits in the character of the noble apostle. This letter deserves to rank with that to the Philippians as a picture in miniature of the perfect saint, saint at once and gentleman. It forms a striking pendant to the Ephesian and Colossian epistles, being as homely and human in its charm as they are sublime and superhuman.

(2) It illustrates Paul's teaching as to *the nullity of worldly rank in the church*. It says by example as Galatians and Colossians by precept: "There is neither slave nor freeman in Christ Jesus." And it indicates

the attitude of Christianity toward slavery and kindred social problems.

(3) In every line and syllable this note betrays Paul's personality. Nothing more genuine was ever written. And it is attached to the Colossian letter so closely, that in effect it *certifies the genuineness* of the latter, which has been much disputed.

Analysis of Philemon

The apostle, after saluting Philemon and his house (Phile. 1–3),

§ 1. *Acknowledges* with gratitude to God *his friend's Christian character and usefulness*, Philemon 4–7.

§ 2. *Intercedes for the fugitive slave*, now a converted man and a brother in Christ, whom it would be a joy to the apostle to see reconciled to his master. What loss Onesimus has inflicted on him Paul undertakes to make good, Philemon 8–21.

§ 3. *Announces his hope of coming soon to Colossae*, and asks for lodging, Philemon 22.

Greetings from his companions and a Benediction complete the letter, Philemon 23–25.

Epistle to the Philippians

The three other letters of this group were all written at one time and sent to the same quarter. Philippians stands apart from the rest. It has points of resemblance to members of the other groups, as well as to those of its own. It reminds us of 1 Thessalonians by its simplicity and warmth of affection; in Philippians 3:1–10 it echoes the teaching of Romans and Galatians; while the language of Philippians 1:23 and 2:16, 17 comes near to that of 2 Timothy 4:6–8 in its anticipation of the writer's death. But the general complexion of the epistle is that of the third group, and the words of Philippians 1:12–14 show that it was written from Paul's prison-lodging at Rome.

Whether Colossians and Ephesians preceded or followed Philippians is a point hard to determine, and of little practical moment. In favor of the latter view, held by Lightfoot and Beet, is the resemblance of Philippians 3:1–10 to Galatians and Romans, whence it is argued that Philippians was the earliest of the prison epistles. In any case, several years intervened between it and Romans, and the appearance of

Judaizers at Philippi at ever so late a period would draw from Paul this sort of condemnation. On the other hand, the words of Philippians 2:23, 24 indicate, more positively than those of Philemon 22, that the prisoner's case is soon to be decided, and Paul must have been at Rome a considerable time for the Philippians to have heard of his necessities there and, after some hindrance and delay (Phil. 4:10, 11), to have sent Epaphroditus for his relief. The epistle cannot have been written in the earliest months of Paul's sojourn at Rome; compare Philippians 1:12–14 to the same effect. We notice, too, that he intends to "send Timothy . . . shortly" to Philippi (Phil. 2:19). Now, Timothy had not left him when he wrote to Colossae (Col. 1:1; Phile. 1). We incline to the usual opinion, that Philippians was the latest epistle of Paul's first captivity. In its unique and splendid theological paragraph (Phil. 2:6–11) this letter gives the crowning expression to the doctrine of the Person of Christ which is taught in the epistle to the Colossians.

Theological teaching is, however, only incidental to the apostle's purpose. This is an epistle of the heart, a true love-letter, full of friendship, gratitude and confidence; it makes those intimate revelations of the soul's history and emotions which the deepest sympathy and mutual affection alone are wont to elicit. While 2 Corinthians discloses the agitations that rent Paul's heart in the great conflict of his life, Philippians shows us the spring of his inward peace and strength. We are admitted to Paul's prison-chamber; we share his holy and joyous meditations and communings with the divine Master; we watch his spirit mellowing to its loveliest ripeness in these quiet autumn hours of life, while patience fulfills in him its perfect work. This epistle holds, as we have already shown, a cardinal place in Paul's spiritual biography.

The Philippians were dearest to Paul of all his children in the faith. Thrice in four chapters he calls them "beloved" (see Phil. 4:1). "From the first day until now" they had entered into his plans and made his cause and his work their own. His fellowship with them was never marred by the offenses and suspicions with which other churches had troubled him (Phil. 1:3–7, 30). On his first mission to Macedonia they sent to help his necessity at Thessalonica more than once, and afterwards, at Corinth, he allowed them to minister to him when he refused contributions from others (Phil. 4:15, 16; cf.

2 Cor. 11:9, 10). Their concern for him now revived (Phil. 4:10); they had wished to send him help before this, but the means were wanting. Their present gift was exceedingly grateful to the afflicted apostle, whose resources they supposed were low, unable as he probably was in imprisonment to carry on with advantage his trade of tent-making, and feeling already the infirmities of age (Phile. 9). But he rejoiced chiefly in the love displayed by his Philippian children, and in the blessing which he was sure God would bestow upon them in return (Phil. 4:17–20). This is the happiest of Paul's letters. "Summa epistolae, *Gaudeo, gaudete*," says sententious Bengel: "*I rejoice, do you rejoice!* is the sum of the letter."

The present from Philippi was sent by the hand of *Epaphroditus*, who fell sick in his journey and had risked his life on the errand (Phil. 2:25–30). He was a minister in the Philippian church, ranking perhaps among its "overseers" (Phil. 1:1); the apostle describes him as "my brother and fellow-worker and fellow-soldier" (cf. Phile. 2), and in virtue of this commission "your messenger (i.e., *delegate* or *emissary*) and minister to my need" (Phil. 2:25). Epaphroditus was greatly attached to his own people and anxious to return; he felt the distress which his illness had caused them. The apostle accordingly sends him home without delay, giving him this letter of acknowledgment to carry with him. His own appeal at the Caesar's court is entering upon a critical stage, so soon as he sees how it will issue, he will send word by Timothy. But he "trust[s] in the Lord" that he will be able himself to come before long (Phil. 2:19–24), a presentiment that we cannot believe was disappointed.

Analysis of Philippians

This epistle has less of definite structure and is more of a free outpouring of the heart than any other. It consists, like 1 Thessalonians, of personal news, blended with exhortation and warning.

After the introduction (Phil. 1:1–11), consisting of Salutation, Thanksgiving, and Prayer (that *knowledge* may be added to love), the writer:

§ 1. Describes *his own position and feelings*, Philippians 1:12–26.

§ 2. Exhorts them to *courage*, in fellowship with himself (Phil. 1:27–30); to *brotherly unity*, Philippians 2:1, 2 (cf. Eph. 4:1–6); to *humility*, after the example of Christ (Phil. 2:3–11), and to *fidelity*, which would ensure his own reward (Phil. 2:12–18).

§ 3. Promises to *send* them *Timothy*, while he *dispatches Epaphroditus* their messenger at once, warmly commending both (Phil. 2:19–30).

§ 4. Warns them *against Judaizers*, and against men of corrupt life; whose glorying in the flesh he contrasts with his own principles and aims. He bids them be followers of him, Philippians 3—4:1 (cf. 2 Cor. 11:16—12:12; Gal. 6:12–14; 1 Thess. 2:1–12). It is here that the apostle so fully opens his heart to us.

§ 5. Exhorts them again to *unity*, appealing in particular to two ladies, Euodia and Syntyché, and a certain Clement (Phil. 4:2, 3); also to *serenity of spirit* (Phil. 4:4–7), and the *just appreciation of every virtue* (Phil. 4:8, 9).

§ 6. Acknowledges *their bounty,* and expresses the emotions it excited in him, Philippians 4:10–20.

Final Greeting and Benediction, Philippians 4:21–23.

We conclude this chapter by a paraphrase of some difficult passages in the above epistles.

Colossians 2:13–15:

"God raised you up, through the resurrection of Christ, from the death of sin and from your unclean Gentile state. He forgave your sins, and nailed to the cross the canceled bill which the Law had against you. At the same time He cast off from Himself the old veil of angelic mediation and made a show of the heavenly powers, who were led along in Christ's triumphal train."

Colossians 2:18:

"Let none defraud you of the heavenly prize (cf. Col. 1:5), though he fain would do it with his humility and his angel-worship, with his vain theorizing based on fancied visions, the creation of a carnal and inflated mind."

Colossians 2:23:

"Rules which have word indeed (*or* show) of wisdom, but nothing more. These rules exhibit a love of worship and a humility that make them plausible, and an outward austerity which sets no honor on the body, while it fails to curb the sinful flesh."

Ephesians 3:14–19:

"May God the Father, whose sons are both in heaven and on earth, give you through His Spirit a strength of soul proportioned to the glory of the revelation He has made to you! May the Christ in all His fullness make His home through faith within your hearts! Thus established in love, you and the whole church will be enabled to comprehend the vast scope and dimensions of the redeeming plan; yes, and you will know the greatness of the love of Christ, though it passes knowledge! Then at last you will be filled, and your nature made complete with all the plenitude of God."

Philippians 2:5–11:

"Let that mind be in you which belongs to those in Christ Jesus. His form of being was divine, but He did not deem His equality of state with God a thing to be clutched at (to be held fast in self-assertion). On the contrary, He laid it all aside; He took the place of a slave, and appeared in human form. He humbled Himself; He proved obedient to the point of death, nay, the death of the cross!

"On this account God has raised Him beyond all height, and has bestowed on Him that unrivaled *name* of His, so that in the name of Jesus 'every knee may bend'—heavenly, earthly, or below the earth—and 'every tongue confess' the LORD JESUS CHRIST to the divine Father's glory!"

The Three
Pastorals

There remain for our consideration among the letters bearing Paul's name the three addressed to Timothy and Titus, which are commonly called *the pastoral epistles*. Followed only by Philemon (and Heb.), they close the canonical order of Paul's epistles; not because of their late date, and certainly not from any doubt of their authenticity, but because these four were written to individuals while the nine preceding them were addressed to churches. There is a distinction, however, in the fact that the note to Philemon is concerned with strictly personal matters, while to Timothy and Titus the apostle writes on the affairs of the church, and in such a way that a great part of his letters might be, and probably were, read in the public assembly. (Observe the *pl.* form of the Benediction in each, and the double Benediction of 2 Tim. 4:22.) The Pastorals are in reality *quasi-public*, or half-public, letters. Still, they were intended in the first instance for ministers, not for churches; they bear on the qualifications and duties belonging to church office and the care of souls. We entitle them accordingly *the ecclesiastical epistles*.

They belong to the close of Paul's ministry, and have throughout, especially 2 Timothy, a *valedictory* character. They are the apostle's farewell to the church, his dying charge to his successors in the gospel ministry. This lends them a peculiar weight and pathos. They exhibit Paul in old age, and on the verge of martyrdom (2 Tim. 4:6). The picture that these letters give us of the circumstances and feelings of the apostle now at his journey's end, slight as it is and obscure in some of its details, is exceedingly precious. It is all that time has left to us.

Object of the Pastorals

Besides the personal interest attaching to these epistles, and besides their important bearing on the constitution of the apostolic church, they throw a striking light upon the progress of heresy in Paul's later days. In certain points, moreover: especially in regard to the divine attributes (1 Tim. 1:17; 4:10; 6:15–18), the sanctity of nature (1 Tim. 4:3–5), the inspiration of Scripture (2 Tim. 3:15–17), the ethical qualities of the Christian life and their connection with evangelical doctrine (1 Tim. 6:11, 12; Titus 2:1—3:11)—they show a further development of his teaching; at any rate, they give it new application and more distinct expression.

The *conservative* tendency which we observed in the last group of letters, now becomes thoroughly pronounced; it was stimulated in the apostle by the speculative and divisive character that marked Gnosticism from the beginning. "Practical piety and correct doctrine form the two poles, equally dominant, of the Pastoral epistles" (Holtzmann). Among the many novel expressions, new to Paul's vocabulary, as we have learned it from the other epistles, none are more characteristic than the words *godliness* (1 Tim. 2:2, 10; 3:16; 4:7, 8, etc.), and *deposit* (of revealed truth: 1 Tim. 6:20; 2 Tim. 1:12, 14).

These words indicate the twofold object which had now become Paul's supreme concern, the burden of his latest thoughts and cares on the church's behalf. This purpose governs and shapes the directions which he gives in Titus 1 and 1 Timothy 3 for the choice of *overseers* (or *elders*) and *deacons*. False and sophistical teachers were imposing themselves on the Christian societies, men such as the apostle had described in Acts 20:29, 30, the Colossian doctor was a sample of them, whose asceticism and scriptural jargon were calculated to impress superficial minds (1 Tim. 1:6, 7; 4:1–3; 6:3–10). They are the forerunners of impostors even more corrupt and dangerous than themselves: so "the Spirit explicitly says" to Paul (1 Tim. 4:1; 2 Tim. 3:1–9; 4:3, 4). In view of this development, and with strong apprehension that these "savage wolves" would seek to prey on the church under the shepherd's garb, the apostle pens the remarkable instructions which lie before us here.

Obviously, they are not intended as a complete description of what the overseers and deacons should be. To the need in its ministry of other, more shining gifts the church was sufficiently alive. What the apostle insists upon is that solid moral qualities shall not be overlooked, nor taken for granted without inquiry, in the appointment of its officers. The danger was lest talent and cleverness should carry the day, and the leadership of the church fall into the hands of men deficient in the elements of a worthy Christian character.

> The prescriptions of these epistles, [as Dr. Kühl aptly says,] bear throughout an eminently practical stamp; they find their characteristic expression in the exhortation to Timothy, *Be thou a pattern of the believers.* The false intellectualism of the errorist is traced to their want of practical piety, and this *eusebeia,* this open sense for the divine, has in turn its practical guarantee in a Christianly moral life. Such piety it is the aim of these writings in their whole tenor to quicken and renew.

The aged apostle bends all his efforts to guard and strengthen the spirit of religion. Himself "ready to be poured out as a drink offering," with his battle fought, his course run, and the great fabric of his doctrine built to its completeness in Christ, his one remaining care is to see the deposit committed to faithful and worthy hands. He desires to leave behind him in the churches he had founded a community so ordered and equipped, so rooted and built in Christ, that it shall be for all time to come a "pillar and support of the truth." To the Christian society thus fully constituted, is committed the mystery of godliness now fully revealed. Such is the situation which the fourth group of the Pauline epistles reveals to us. They are, in effect, the last will and testament of the apostle of the Gentiles. They stand related to Paul's ministry somewhat as does the valedictory prayer of John 17 to the teaching of Jesus. The servant seems, in some sort, to be saying as his Master: "The words which Thou gavest Me I have given to them. . . . The glory which Thou hast given Me I have given to them, that they may be one . . . perfected in unity" (John 17:8, 22, 23; cf. 1 Tim. 1:11–18; 2 Tim. 1:8–14; 2:2, 8–10; see also Eph. 4:11–13).

The Pastorals and the Earlier Epistles

In the epistle to the *Ephesians* the letters to Timothy and Titus find the most definite and numerous points of attachment among Paul's earlier writings. Those who condemn these epistles as unauthentic, are commonly obliged to place Ephesians in the same category. In Ephesians the step is completed by which we pass from the idea of the local to that of the ecumenical church. In it we see already many buildings combined to form "a holy temple in the Lord" (Eph. 2:21, 22); in other words, the church has taken on a *connectional* in addition to its congregational character. There also we find a collective and graduated ministry in existence, bestowed by the Head of the church for the perfecting of His saints, for the protection of the community in its infant and imperfect state from the assaults of error, and for the development and utilization of the various powers and capacities diffused through its individual membership (Eph. 4:11–16). The Pastorals do but expand and apply the conception of the church and its ministry which in essentials is already present here. From the thought of the "large house" unfolded in Ephesians we pass to that of the "vessels" of its furniture, their qualities and uses, and the solemn responsibilities which accrue to them. Their importance lies in the greatness of the church they serve, and hers in the greatness of the truth she holds in trust for mankind (1 Tim. 3:15, 16; 2 Tim. 2:19–21).

With *Colossians* the Pastorals are connected as closely, if not so obviously, as with Ephesians. Compare 1 Timothy 4:3–5 with Colossians 2:20–23—1 Timothy 2:5–7 with Colossians 1:15–23; 2:9–15— 1 Timothy 6:3, 4, 20, 21; 2 Timothy 2:16; 3:6; Titus 1:13–16 with Colossians 2:2–4, 8, 16, 22, and it will be seen that, with considerable variety, there was a fundamental resemblance in the errors combated by the earlier and later writings. In both cases the false doctrine denounced was Judaistic in complexion, and yet radically different from the Pharisaic legalism of the Galatian "troublers." Contempt for the body, denial of God's part in creation and in the physical order of the world, underlay both types of heresy. Christ's mediatorial rights were invaded and limited by both.

But the new Gnosticizing "deceitful scheming" (Eph. 4:14) now infringed openly upon the prerogatives of God. The "fables and logomachies" of these theosophists sapped the basis of religion. Theories that separate God from nature and body from spirit, are in the long run fatal to piety. They tend to dissolve the religious conception of life and to destroy "faith and a good conscience," godliness and virtue, both at once. The other common features we mark are the intellectual pretension, the argumentative style, the domineering attitude and the self-seeking spirit of this class of teachers. In the errorists of the Pastorals, side by side with the rigorism of the Colossian teacher, symptoms begin to appear of the license which this type of doctrine inevitably breeds (1 Tim. 6:5–10; 2 Tim. 3:1–8, Titus 1:12–16). The "Jewish myths" and "endless genealogies" alluded to in 1 Timothy 1:4 and Titus 1:14, cannot be explained with certainty. Probably they were concerned with the different ranks and supposed families (cf. Eph. 3:15) of the angels, whom we find the Colossian teacher already worshiping at the expense of Christ. At a very early time Jewish mysticism by its allegorical interpretations deduced an elaborate angelology from the Old Testament.

We have already pointed out, in the last chapter, the link of connection between these letters and *Philippians* in their similar references to the apostle's death. This he contemplates as possible in Philippians 1:20–23, 2:17, but in 2 Timothy 4:5–8, 18, it is inevitable and imminent. There is a further resemblance between this and the third group of epistles generally, in the manner in which the apostle writes of his imprisonment and his sufferings in the cause of Christ: compare 2 Timothy 1:11, 12; 2:9, 10; 4:17 with Colossians 1:24–28; 4:3, 4; Ephesians 3:1–5, 13; 6:19, 20; Philippians 1:16.

In one singular passage, 1 Timothy 1:8–11, we have an echo of the apostle's bold doctrine of *Galatians* and *Romans* concerning the design of the Mosaic Law, which, he shows, was intended as a whip for the sinner, not a yoke for the saint: see Galatians 3:10, 19; Romans 3:19, 20; 4:15; 5:20, and compare Romans 6:14; 7:5, 6; 8:2. The phrase "who gave Himself as *a ransom for all*" (1 Tim. 2:6), supplies the term which brings to its final expression the doctrine of the vicarious sacrifice taught in the evangelical epistles. And the doctrinal paragraphs of Titus 2: 11–14; 3:4–7 unfold in ripened and rounded form the whole Pauline plan of salvation. In the same connection we note the solemn introduction to the epistle to Titus (1:1–4), which reminds us both of the opening and the closing words of Romans.

With *1 Corinthians* we find two incidental, but not unimportant points of connection: (1) the denial of a bodily resurrection on the part of "Hymenaeus and Philetus" (2 Tim. 2:18; cf. 1 Cor. 15), made doubtless in the interests of a false spiritualism, and (2) the care taken to regulate the position and behavior of women in the church: compare 1 Timothy 2:9–15; 3:11; 5:3–16; 2 Timothy 3:6, 7, Titus 2:3–5 with 1 Corinthians 11:2–16; 14:34–36. This subject had at different times considerably exercised the apostle's mind.

Finally, when we compare *the first group* of the Epistles with the last, we find that they have one cardinal theme in common, namely, that of the Second Coming. This is, in a sense, the alpha and omega of Paul's teaching. Many charges have passed over him in the fifteen years intervening. He no longer expects, nor even desires, to see in the flesh his Lord's return. But he is nonetheless "looking for and hasting the coming of the day of God" (2 Pet. 3:12). The appearing of Christ in His divine glory is "the blessed hope" which all believers are awaiting (Titus 2:13). "In the presence of God and of Christ Jesus, who is to judge the living and dead, and by His appearing and His kingdom": the apostle addresses his final charge to Timothy (2 Tim. 4:1, 2, 5). As the time of his departure approached, the advent of the Lord Jesus shone forth upon Paul's spirit with new brightness and shed its glory over the darkness of the grave and the last steps of his earthly journey. Compare Philippians 3:20, 21; Romans 8:18–25; 2 Corinthians 4:16; 5:10, for the like association of thought at an earlier time.

Authenticity of the Pastoral Epistles

A thorough study of these and other links of connection between the Pastorals and the earlier letters will, we think, deprive of their force the arguments that are urged by many critical writers against the claim they make to be the work of Paul. It is true that there is no place for these writings within the limits of his career as known to us from Acts, and that all other contemporary evidence has disappeared. But the narrative of Acts closes in such a way as to allow, if not actually to suggest, the probability that his life was extended beyond the two years there assigned to his imprisonment at Rome (Acts 28:30, 31). There is nothing whatever in Luke's narrative to discountenance the belief, favored by tradition, that the apostle was at last acquitted of the charge on which he had appealed to Caesar, and set free to resume his labors for another term. There is not a shred of historical evidence *against* the letters. The witness of the early church to their place in the New Testament Canon and their Pauline authorship is as clear, full, and un-hesitating as that given to the other epistles. It is only on grounds of internal criticism that objections of real weight can be raised.

So far as these criticisms are drawn from the *contents* of the epis-tles, from the novelty of the topics of which they treat, from the ad-vanced development of the errors, they oppose and of the church system which they imply, we have already met them by anticipation. The condition of things with which Paul had now to deal arose, as we have tried to show, out of that described in his previous letters; the doctrinal and administrative instructions of those letters are the nat-ural sequel of Paul's earlier teaching and missionary work. Things had indeed marched quickly in the four or five years separating this group from the last, but it was an advance, alike on the side of attack and de-fense, upon the lines already laid down, and the rate of movement is not more rapid than we might expect in the early days of the church, and in a time of so much mental activity and unrest.

The objections drawn from the *language and style* of the epistles are more plausible. In these thirteen chapters, of less than the ordinary length, there are, excluding proper names, 171 Greek words used nowhere else in the New Testament, an average of thirteen to the chapter. To a large extent, these are accounted for by the peculiar sub-ject-matter; Paul uses new names in writing of new things. The apostle's vocabulary was uncommonly fresh; he was inventive and orig-inal in language, and the habit of using novel and singular expressions grew upon him. In 1 and 2 Thessalonians we find five *hapax-legomena* (i.e., words confined to these writings) to the chapter; in Philippians, an epistle of similar character but written ten years later, there are ten! In general, a careful examination of the lexical and grammatical features of the Pastorals leads us to conclude that they are Pauline in the basis and structure of their language, and that they carry further, down to a later stage, some of Paul's most characteristic mannerisms, his fondness for original compound terms, and his habit of stringing together participial and relative clauses to an indefinite length, and of breaking off his longer sentences unfinished (see e.g. 1 Tim. 6:13–16; 2 Tim. 1:3–12; Titus 1:1–4; 2:11–14). The frequency of medical terms is naturally explained by Luke's companionship in Paul's later years (2 Tim. 4:11; cf. Col. 4:14). And occasional Latinisms betray the effect on Paul's speech of his residence in the West.

In wealth of argument, in fire and vehemence, we admit that these epistles do not compare with the great epistles of the legalist controversy. Paul did not speak or write always at the same high pitch, nor do the subjects he is here concerned with call for the same mental effort. Writing to his intimates, his companions and sons in the gospel, the apostle has no need to expatiate upon doctrine, to prove or defend the great principles of his theology. These appear in the Pastorals as a conquest securely won, a foundation now fixed and firmly laid. The Thessalonian epistles, as we saw, are on a more ordinary level in this respect than those of the following group: when those letters were written, the legalistic agitation had not commenced; by this time it had comparatively subsided.

These are the works of the apostle's old age. The fiery vigor of his prime is gone. But in its place there is a holy tranquillity, a tender, pensive strain of recollection and a rich sunset glow inexpressibly beautiful and touching. It is the veteran apostle to whom we listen, the sun of whose glorious day is sinking to its rest. This mellowed style, this softer and calmer tone was already discernible in the letters of the third group. They are the afternoon, as these are the evening epistles. If there are the signs of age in these writings, it is that of "such a person as Paul, the aged" (Phile. 9).

Order and Date of the Three Epistles

Writing to Colossae and Philippi during his previous imprisonment, Paul expressed his intention to visit those towns immediately upon his release (Phil. 2:24; Phile. 22). He would naturally make it his first business to revisit the old churches, and the districts in which he had formerly labored. Then the way would be open for that voyage to Spain which he contemplated six years before (Rom. 15:24). Whether it was upon his way back from Spain or under some other circumstances, we find from the letter to *Titus* that Paul during this period, shortly before he wrote that epistle, had conducted a mission in Crete, where he left Titus in charge to organize the churches there established, churches in which from the beginning a Gnostic leaven had been at work (Titus 1:5–14). He writes, apparently, in the course of the summer, intending to winter at Nicopolis, the port of Epirus, opposite to Italy. There Titus is desired to meet him (Titus 3:12).

Turning to *2 Timothy* (2 Tim. 4:10), manifestly the last of the three, we find that Titus has gone "to Dalmatia," which lay to the north of Nicopolis, while Tychicus had been sent not to Crete (Titus 3:12) but to Ephesus, from which place (cf. 1 Tim. 1:3) Paul expects his dear child Timothy soon to come to him, now a prisoner at Rome (2 Tim. 4:10, 12). "Make every effort to come to me soon; . . . to come before winter," pleads the old, forsaken man (2 Tim. 4:9, 21), and he asks Timothy to bring "the cloak . . . left at Troas," which the prisoner would miss in the cold days of winter. So near are these two letters to each other, that the "winter" of Titus 3:12 must surely have been the same as that of 2 Timothy 4:21. Second Timothy 4:13, 20 allude to the writer having been recently at Miletus, also at Troas, and (seemingly) at Corinth, points which indicate a journey westwards from Asia Minor through Macedonia and Achaia, such as would bring Paul to Nicopolis. During this journey, soon after he had written to Titus, Paul was arrested, on some charge in which "Alexander the coppersmith" (of Ephesus) played a chief part (2 Tim. 4:14, 15); he was hurried to Rome for a second trial, under circumstances likely to issue in his condemnation and death. It must be remembered that in the interval subsequent to the apostle's release the Christians had become objects of Nero's fury, and the frightful persecution of autumn 64 had taken place at Rome. The epistle to Titus and the second to Timothy we assign to the last year of Paul's life, the latter half of A.D. 66, or 67.[2]

First Timothy was the earliest of the three, being written in the course of the journey above referred to, and in all probability from Macedonia. "I urged you," writes the apostle, "upon my departure for Macedonia, remain on at Ephesus" (1 Tim. 1:3). It is inferred from these words that Paul had just been at Ephesus, and had left Timothy behind him there, as he had left Titus at Crete (Titus 1:5). But these two cases are very different, and the language the apostle uses in the two letters is different. For our part, we do not believe that Paul ever set foot in Ephesus after he left the city as recorded in Acts 20 (cf. Acts 20:25). He departed then in peril of his life, shaken both in mind

---

2. The later this date, the better we can account for the absence of allusion in the Pastorals to the persecution of the year 64 and the crisis then befalling the church.

and body. It was "the Jews from Asia" who attempted to murder him in Jerusalem, seeing with him "Trophimus the Ephesian" (Acts 21:27–29). Alexander, the Jewish craftsman of Ephesus (Acts 19:33, 34), was at the bottom of the conspiracy now formed against him, which in the event proved fatal. The "Asiarchs," his friends in the first instance, seem afterwards to have betrayed him (cf. Acts 19:31 and 2 Tim. 1:15; 4:16). Ephesus was for Paul a fatal place, and he may well have been forbidden of the Holy Spirit, from the time of Acts 20:35, to return there. What he really says in 1 Timothy 1:3 is: "I urged you *upon my departure* for Macedonia, *remain on* at Ephesus."

We gather that the apostle met Timothy, who had been for some time stationed at Ephesus, not very far from the city, possibly at Miletus (2 Tim. 4:20; cf. Acts 20:17), and gave him instructions respecting his duties there, which he repeats and enlarges in this letter written shortly after the interview. Timothy was very unwilling to remain at this trying post; he parted from the apostle in tears (2 Tim. 1:4). His discouragement became extreme after Paul's departure (2 Tim. 1:7, 8; 2:1–13, 4:5), and he was even tempted to give up his work. Some critics indeed infer from the language of the second epistle that, when Paul wrote it, Timothy had actually retreated from Ephesus, but the reference of 2 Timothy 4:19 (cf. 2 Tim. 1:16–18) speaks against that. Evidently he was wavering and in danger of drawing back, if he had not actually done so. Had Paul himself visited the church of Ephesus, he would have dealt in person with the matters that he now commits to his assistant; in any case, we should have had some allusion to the circumstances of the visit. The excommunication inflicted upon "Hymenaeus and Alexander" (1 Tim. 1:20) may have been pronounced from a distance, as easily as that directed against the Corinthian profligate in 1 Corinthians 5:3–5.

The most likely theory of Paul's movements at this time is as follows. Returning from Crete in the spring of A.D. 66 or 67, he voyaged along the coast of Asia Minor, where he touched at Miletus, sending for Timothy from Ephesus, as he had done for the Ephesian elders nine years before on his way to Jerusalem. In this interview he persuaded Timothy, much against his will, to remain in Ephesus for a while longer, until he should himself return to Asia (1 Tim. 3:14, 15), and promised to send him before long a letter of full instructions. Thence Paul continued his voyage northwards, through Troas to Macedonia.

There he wrote to Timothy, and shortly after in a similar strain to Titus, who was engaged in Crete. From Macedonia he went on to Corinth, intending to make Nicopolis the goal of his year's travels, but was seized before the summer was over, and carried a prisoner to Rome to meet his death.

The three letters resemble each other and differ from all the rest to such a degree, that we cannot be mistaken in treating them as closely continuous and separated from the previous group by a considerable interval. Titus differs from the other two less than they from each other, and claims a place between them. Like 1 Timothy it is disciplinary and ethical in contents, while the interest of 2 Timothy is mainly personal.

Analysis of the Pastorals

These epistles are loose in structure; they have the freedom and spontaneity of oral conversation. There is, however, something of a definite order in 1 Timothy and Titus.

In 1 TIMOTHY, after a brief salutation (1 Tim. 1:1, 2), the apostle:

§ 1. Reminds Timothy of *the charge laid upon him*, especially to inculcate right views concerning the Law, in opposition to Jewish fables, 1 Timothy 1:3–11, 18–20. This charge he enforces by reference to *his own ministry*, which occasions an outburst of praise, 1 Timothy 1:12–17.

§ 2. He gives *directions as to the conduct of public prayer*, and *the deportment of women* in connection therewith, 1 Timothy 2.

§ 3. He gives *instructions respecting the appointment of overseers and deacons*, 1 Timothy 3:1–13, inferring the importance of their choice from the greatness of the church, 1 Timothy 3:14–16.

§ 4. He *warns Timothy against heretical teachers*, 1 Timothy 4:1–5, and again in 1 Timothy 6:3–10, 20, 21.

§ 5. He *exhorts him as to the personal character* he must maintain and the line of conduct he must follow, in contrast with these men, 1 Timothy 4:6–16; 6:11–16.

§ 6. He *instructs him as to his behavior toward particular classes* in the church: the old and the young, aged and younger widows, ruling elders and those under accusation, household slaves, and rich men, 1 Timothy 5:1— 6:2; 6:17–19.

The letter to Titus is concerned with a state of things in Crete similar to that existing at Ephesus, but less complicated. It falls into two divisions, after a full exordium (Titus 1—3) reminding us of Romans 1:1-7.

§ 1. Concerning *church order*, as regards:

(1) the qualifications of its officers, Titus 1:5-9;

(2) the character of its disturbers, Titus 1:10-16.

§ 2. Concerning *Christian conduct*, in relation:

(1) to *family life*, Titus 2,

(2) to *civil and social life*, Titus 3:1-8, the motives appealed to being derived from the first principles of the gospel. (These two chs. give us invaluable hints on the method of Christian ethics.)

(3) To *heretical persons*, whom Titus is to shun, after repeated warning, Titus 3:9-11.

The Conclusion, Titus 3:12-15, contains interesting personal references, which go far to verify the genuineness of the letter.

SECOND TIMOTHY throughout consists of exhortation and appeal. The apostle, after saluting Timothy (2 Tim. 1:1, 2), and thanking God for all that his "beloved son" had been to him (2 Tim. 1:3-5):

§ 1. *Exhorts him to courage*, in view of the divine glory of the gospel, and in spite of his own desertion and disgrace, 2 Timothy 1:6—2:13.

He bids him, by the way, *maintain the exact form of apostolic teaching*, and commit it in turn to worthy and competent men (2 Tim. 1:13, 14; 2:2).

§ 2. *To faithfulness* in the maintenance of sound doctrine: (1) against *the idle debates and ungodly life* of heretical teachers, with whose behavior he compares his own (2 Tim. 3:10, 11); (2) faithfulness the more needful as *his own course is nearly run*, 2 Timothy 2:14—4:8.

§ 3. He concludes by *begging Timothy to come* to him *soon*, describing his lonely condition, yet unshaken confidence in his heavenly Master, 2 Timothy 4:9-18.

In *the final greetings* new names appear, two of them Roman (Pudens and Claudia), and one, Linus, which figures in the list of the first overseers of Rome. The personal references in 2 Timothy 4 are the most numerous and varied that occur in any epistle except that to the Romans.

The apostle passes from our view with the double Benediction on his lips: *The Lord be with your spirit. Grace be with you.*

Paraphrases

First Timothy 1:3–5: "(I write now) in accordance with the request I made when on my way to Macedonia, that you should remain in Ephesus. I wished you to charge certain persons to give up their strange teaching and their taste for fables and spun-out genealogies, which raise discussions, but do not further God's dispensation of grace to the men of faith. Love, verily, is the practical end of all our teaching, the love that comes of a pure heart and a good conscience and undissembled faith."

First Timothy 3:14–16: "I write these things hoping indeed to come quickly to you. But I may be delayed, and I wish you to know how you should behave yourself within God's house. For it is, I say, the church of the living God; it is the pillar and basis on which rests the truth. And the greatness of that truth, that mystery committed to the men of God (Eph. 3:5; 1 Cor. 2:6–16), who can deny? the mystery of Him who was manifested in the fleshly sphere, was justified in the spiritual (Rom. 1:4; 1 Cor. 2:8, 14), appeared to the angels; was proclaimed among the Gentiles, was believed in the world, was taken up in glory!" (For the connection of the last clauses, cf. 1 Pet. 1:7, 8, 20, 21.)

Titus 3:3–7: "There was a time when we, too, were senseless, disobedient, wandering from the way, in bondage to manifold lusts and pleasures, living in envy and malice, hateful and hating each other. But when our Savior God displayed His kindness and love to men, then indeed He saved us, not by works that we ourselves had done as a matter of righteousness, but in the way of His mercy, by means of the laver of new birth and the renewing power of the Holy Spirit (John 3:5). This He poured out richly upon us through Jesus Christ our Savior, to the end that we might be justified by His grace and made heirs in hope of life eternal."

Second Timothy 4:6–8: "For my life is a libation ready for the sacrifice. It is time to break up my tent (2 Cor. 5:1; 2 Pet. 1:14). The good fight I have fought out; I have run the race; I have kept the faith to the end. For the rest, there is in store for me the crown of righteousness, which the Lord will give me in the great day, that righteous Judge! nor to me alone, but to all that have set their love on His appearing."

General Survey

"I have fought the good fight, I have finished the course, I have kept the faith," such are the apostle's last words to the church through Timothy (2 Tim. 4:7). Through every land from Syria to Spain, through every class of Gentile society from the slave to the emperor, the apostle of the Gentiles has proclaimed his message. This external progress was attended by a corresponding internal development. In his spiritual experience Paul had penetrated to the depths of the mystery of Christ, while his inspired logic and force of character had won for the gospel a decisive victory over Jewish reaction and the antagonism of philosophical thought. The Pauline churches, as the apostle left them at the close of his ministry, were the result and the witness of this manifold activity. "I was appointed," he says, "a preacher and an apostle . . . as a teacher of the Gentiles in faith and truth" (1 Tim. 2:7; 2 Tim. 1:11), and he has made full proof of this ministry. "You are the seal of my apostleship," he could say to Gentile Christendom, "in the Lord. . . . (1 Cor. 9:2) In Christ Jesus, I became your father through the gospel" (1 Cor. 4:15). Paul sees his message accepted and his teaching embodied in the existence of the church throughout the Roman empire. The permanence of the gospel and its propagation among mankind are guaranteed. "A pillar and support" are set up, on which, he is well assured, "the truth" will stand fast forever (1 Tim. 3:15).

Along three distinct lines we may, therefore, trace the general course of Paul's apostolic work: (1) The progress of *his evangelistic mission;* (2) the development of *his theological doctrine,* and (3) *the building up of the church* under his care.

Paul's Work as an Evangelist

Before the apostle settled at Antioch (A.D. 43), he had preached the gospel in Damascus and Jerusalem, and for several years in his native province of Cilicia (Gal. 1:21; cf. Acts 9:30). But it was at Antioch that the Gentile mission was fairly commenced (Acts 13:1–3). Here the church, in its true idea as a worldwide community, was instituted. To Antioch Cypriote and Cyrenian Jews "began speaking *to the Greeks* also, preaching the Lord Jesus" (Acts 11:19–28); "the disciples were first called *Christians* in Antioch." The new name signalized the appearance on the platform of history of the new community. Derived from a Hebrew root (*Messiah*) translated into Greek (*Christos*), and furnished with a Latin ending (*Christian*)—the title being coined, as Ewald reasonably conjectures, by the Roman authorities of Antioch when they first took cognizance of the disciples of Jesus—it precisely characterized the Judaeo-Gentile society over which Barnabas and Paul presided at Antioch, and the word quickly passed into general and settled use.

In and around Antioch Paul labored for some six years (A.D. 43—49). It was there that he rose to the ascendancy which marked him out as apostle "to the uncircumcised" (Gal. 2:1–10; cf. Acts 15), as he had been already designated by "a revelation of Jesus Christ" (Gal. 1:11–16). There, at a later time, his apostleship was signally vindicated by the reproof administered to Peter for his Judaistic lapse (Gal. 2:11–21). The church of Antioch laid its hands upon him, "urging [him] to continue in the grace of God" (Acts 13:43) for his wider mission (Acts 13:1–3). There he returned with the tidings of success (Acts 14:26–28; again in Acts 18:22, 23), regarding Antioch, as we imagine, even to the last as his headquarters and the nursing-mother of Gentile Christendom.

From this center his activity proceeded in ever-widening circles. The first recorded missionary circuit, of Barnabas and Paul, extended to the center of Asia Minor. The second tour was designed to embrace the west of the peninsula. But the apostle's course was diverted to Europe, and Macedonia and Greece next heard his message. The third missionary journey completed and consolidated the work of the second. Ephesus, mid-way between Antioch and Corinth, was occupied for Christ, and the province of Asia was planted with churches. Meanwhile the Judaistic reaction, with its "gospel contrary to that which you received" (Gal. 1:8, 9), was repelled after a violent struggle. When at the end of this period (A.D. 56) the apostle writes to Rome, he regards his mission in the east of the empire as already fulfilled (Rom. 15:19–24), and he is setting his face towards Italy and Spain.

The next stage in his career finds him arrived at Rome, but far otherwise than he expected, "an ambassador in chains" (Eph. 6:20). Yet this captivity, which appeared so disastrous, had "turned out for the greater progress of the gospel." Paul was free to preach to all in the city who came to him, and his position gave him the means, which otherwise would have been wanting, to reach the army and the imperial court (Phil. 1:12, 13; 4:22). He fulfilled, as we believe, his intention of preaching in Spain, during the interval between his first and second imprisonment. Syria had heard; Spain had heard, and now, to crown all, he had borne witness before Caesar and the majesty of Rome (Acts 9:15; 23:11). It is a sign to him that "the time of [his] departure has come" (2 Tim. 4:6).

Thus in one wave after another the gospel tidings had been carried, spreading farther and rising higher as it swept through Syria, Asia Minor, Macedonia, Greece, Italy, and Spain. Antioch, Iconium, Galatia, Troas, Thessalonica, Corinth, Ephesus, Rome mark the steps of Paul's triumphant progress.

The Growth of Paul's Doctrine

The distance between Jerusalem and Rome is a type of the interval that separates Peter's sermon on the day of Pentecost from the finished doctrine of the great epistles. The "salvation . . . from the Jews" has now become the possession of mankind. There was in all this a true development, an *unfolding of* the gospel of Jesus Christ, as the Master Himself had left it, to the conscience and faith of the Gentile world. The reproach of innovation cast upon Paul by the Judaists of his own time, and which modern critics have taken up again as though it were a tribute to his genius, alleging that he effected a radical transformation

in the primitive Christian faith and gave it a new spirit and power—
that Paul, and not Jesus, is in effect the author of Christianity, is utterly false. The apostle would have regarded it with horror. His
greatness is that of a servant and disciple. The seed of the word of
Christ falling upon his fertile and daring mind, developed itself with
marvelous potency and bore fruit of incomparable richness, but it was
the fruit of no other seed than this. Neither Judaism nor Hellenism
had contributed to it anything essential. The apostolic theology existed in germ and purpose already in the teaching of Jesus. The
foundation that Paul laid was Jesus Christ, and "no . . . other"
(1 Cor. 3:11); the gospel that he preached, from first to last, he "received from the Lord," "through a revelation of Jesus Christ" (1 Cor.
11:23; Gal. 1:12).

This was Paul's absolute conviction, and it is confirmed by a
just analysis of his writings and comparison of their contents with the
doctrine of the four Evangelists. However far the apostle advanced in
thought and in experience, Christ was still infinitely beyond him, and
he was but "press[ing] on . . . to lay hold of that for which also I was
laid hold of by Christ Jesus" (Phil. 3:12.) The more deeply he explored
the divine mystery, the more he was overwhelmed by its vastness, by
the sense of "the unfathomable riches of Christ" (Eph. 3:8). He was
transported with "the surpassing value of knowing Christ," (Phil. 3:8)
and the greatness of His love that "surpasses knowledge" (Eph. 3:19).
With such an object of pursuit, the apostle felt that his knowledge
could only be partial, open to constant enlargement and advance.
"Not that I have already obtained it," he seems to say at every point,
"or have already become perfect" (Phil. 3:12). We cannot read Paul's
epistles in the order of their composition without observing this
growth and expansion of his doctrine. We find in them a march of
thought no less signal than the visible progress of his missionary career. Alike in theological knowledge and in spiritual attainment, un-
ceasingly he "press[es] on toward the goal" (Phil. 3:14). The two were
as inseparable as were his intellect and heart. Both are embraced in
that one desire of his: "that I may know Him, and the power of His
resurrection and the fellowship of His sufferings" (Phil. 3:10).

The four groups of the Epistles, broadly considered, present four
successive phases of the apostle's teaching. Throughout we find variety, elasticity, logical development, adaptation to changing condi-

tions, and at the same time an entire unity of organic life and mental structure. Of his epistles one may say, what he said of the greatly differing members of the church in Corinth: "We, who are many, are one body in Christ" (Rom. 12:5).

When the earliest of the extant letters were written to the Thessalonians (in A.D. 50 or 51), Paul had already completed half his course. His mind is mature, his theology wrought out in its main ideas and applications. Whatever new developments it may henceforth receive, in whatever altered forms he may afterwards administer the grace of God to suit the growing demands of the church and the shifting assaults of its enemies, the system of truth inculcated in these first letters is held fast to the end. All that Paul subsequently taught is contained there virtually and by implication.

These epistles, read along with his discourses in Acts, exhibit his teaching in its *missionary* aspect, as it first came into contact with pagan thought, and in the form which it took in the minds of men newly converted from heathenism. Two doctrines, we have seen, are especially conspicuous at this epoch: that of *the true character of God,* in contrast with idols, and that of *Jesus the Messiah and Son of God,* who would quickly return in glory as the righteous judge of the world and deliverer of His faithful people (1 Thess. 1:9, 10, etc.). The Godhead of the Lord Jesus is implied, especially in the prayers addressed to Him along with the Father (1 Thess. 3:11–13; 2 Thess. 2:16, 17).

On two main facts the faith of Paul's Thessalonian converts rested: "We believe that *Jesus died, and rose again*" (1 Thess. 4:14). They are spoken of throughout as "believers," or "those who believed," for faith is the root and spring of their life in the Spirit, it is the reception of God's word, the surrender and union of the soul to Christ (see especially 1 Thess. 2:13; 2 Thess. 1:10; 2:13).

Christ's death was the means of salvation, appointed by God; it brings men deliverance from the divine anger merited by their sins, a deliverance whose full fruition they will enjoy at their Deliverer's return (1 Thess. 5:8–10; 1:10; 2 Thess. 1:7–12; 2:13, 14). His resurrection raises them through faith to a fellowship with Him which survives the grave, and which at His advent will enter upon its consummated form (1 Thess. 4:13–18; 5:10). Add to this the doctrine of *the Holy Spirit,* the supreme gift of God and the element of our fellowship with

Christ, felt as an inward life and fire in the spirit of men, giving strength to those who speak and joy to those who suffer for Christ, sanctifying the body no less than the soul of the believer (1 Thess. 1:5, 6; 4:3–8; 5:19, 20, 23; 2 Thess. 2:13), and we have in these simple letters the kernel and substance of Paul's conception of Christianity. A number of his most characteristic expressions are already here: such as the trilogy of "faith, love, and hope," the "calling" and "election" of believers on the part of God, the "grace of God" viewed as the source of our salvation in Christ and of every personal blessing and favor, "the peace of God" as the center and sum of blessedness.

The principle of *the believer's fellowship with the Lord Jesus Christ in the Spirit*—a fellowship in His life, through His death—is seen to be from the first the center of Paul's theology. It is the keynote of the melody, heard through all its variations, the fundamental point to which the apostle perpetually returns and from which the entire development of his doctrine, whether speculative or practical, may be traced. This truth was to Paul the life of life; it was the secret of the ages, the spring of immortality. He carried its mystery within his own breast (Gal. 1:16; 2:20; Col. 1:25–29; 1 Thess. 5:10).

In 1 and 2 Thessalonians and 1 Corinthians, written when it was not yet revealed to the apostle that he must die before the Lord's return, "the last things" of Christian teaching loom impressively upon us. From the beginning we look straight on to the end; no intervening object detains the eye. The arena of the church's long conflict and discipline is not yet opened. Earthly relations, duties of family and civil life, are of transient importance (1 Cor. 7:29–31). The Lord's return in glory, the resurrection of the dead and the rapture of the living saints, with the revelation of the Lawless One and the manifestation of his Satanic power preceding Christ's descent from heaven, these are the things which for the time possess the thoughts of the church, to a degree to which they have never done at any subsequent period.

The bent of the apostle's teaching in the second group of letters is determined by *the outbreak of the Judaistic controversy*. Truths which he had hitherto delivered in simple didactic form, are in Galatians and Romans expounded and demonstrated in their full theological import. The doctrines of Grace are unfolded and defined. Held, as it were, in solution in Paul's previous teaching and that of the other apostles, the theology of the cross is precipitated by the shock of this contention, and crystallizes into its theoretic form. The apostle's conceptions of the nature and extent of human sin, of the meaning of the death of Christ and its relation to God's law and to His love, of the sole efficacy of faith in man's salvation, of the divine sonship of believers, of his personal vocation as apostle to the Gentiles, of the position and destiny of national Israel, these are the subjects that now occupy the field of view. The *atonement of the cross* and *justification by faith* form the center round which everything moves.

These truths have an underlying experimental basis in the union of the soul with Christ crucified and risen (Rom. 6:4; 2 Cor. 5:14, 15; Gal. 2:20). This governing idea is now expanded and applied in all directions: negatively, as it involves our deliverance from the law of sin and death, as it puts an end to all legal justification and condemns every attempt to establish one's own righteousness, and positively, as it brings with it full devotion to God's service, conformity to the image of His Son, possession of His Spirit, and the attainment by man, both in spirit and body, of the heritage of life eternal.

The kingdom of grace is thus extended over the whole domain of life. It embraces all the nations and all the ages of time, from Adam downward; it dominates all the passions of the heart, and "captivates every thought to the obedience of Christ" (see 2 Cor. 10:5). It triumphs over evil in every field of conflict, so that "where sin increased, grace abounded all the more, that as sin reigned in death, even so grace might reign through righteousness to eternal life through Jesus Christ our Lord" (Rom. 5:20, 21). "But thanks be to God," well may the apostle say, "who always leads us in His triumph in Christ, and manifests through us the sweet aroma of the knowledge of Him in every place" (2 Cor. 2:14). The advance of the evangelical principle in these epistles, its logical and experimental vindication, its mastery of the empire of thought and conscience, are even more triumphant than was its visible progress along the Mediterranean shores.

The letters to the Galatians and Romans have established once for all the sovereignty of grace in religion. Side by side with these stand the two letters to the Corinthians, where the new spirit of evangelical life comes into conflict with manifold forms of social evil, with the impurities, disorders, and rivalries infesting a church not sufficiently weaned from heathenism, whose members "are you not fleshly, and are you not walking like mere men?" (1 Cor. 3:3). At Corinth the combined influence of the Judaistic agitation and of vicious pagan antecedents and surroundings threatened a complete destruction of the work of grace. These influences the apostle combats with one single weapon: all the practical difficulties of the Corinthian church he deals with upon one principle, that of the Christian's living union with Christ. "You were called," he writes, "into fellowship with His Son, Jesus Christ our Lord. . . . (1 Cor. 1:9) What harmony has Christ with Belial? (2 Cor. 6:15) . . . You cannot drink of the cup of the Lord, and the cup of demons! (1 Cor. 10:21) . . . Or do you not know that your body is a temple of the Holy Spirit who is in you? (1 Cor. 6:19) . . . Has Christ been divided? (1 Cor. 1:13) . . . All the members of the body, though they are many, are one body, so also is Christ" (1 Cor. 12:12). Similarly he declares to the Galatians: "For in Christ Jesus neither circumcision nor uncircumcision means anything (Gal. 5:6). . . . For you were called to freedom, brethren . . . through love serve one another"(Gal. 5:13). We see already that the Pauline conception of fellowship with Christ is destined to have momentous and far-reaching ethical consequences. By regenerating the individual heart it will transform the face of society.

The letters of the third group serve to carry out this root idea of life in Christ, in the direction we have just intimated. It is not the individual man alone who is in spirit and body a temple of the Holy Spirit, but "you also are *being built together* into a dwelling of God in the Spirit" (Eph. 2:22). The apostle speaks throughout "with reference to *Christ and the church.*" The creation in Christ of a new humanity, in which Jew and Gentile coalesce and are reconciled to each other as to God (Eph. 2:15–18), "the summing up of all things in Christ" (Eph. 1:10), "the eternal purpose" (Eph. 3:11) with its "breadth and length," its, "height and depth" (Eph. 3:18) embracing all men and all times—nay, all worlds—these are the objects of Paul's sublime prison meditations.

In seeking a basis for the vast construction into which the church has grown before his eyes, and in tracing out the scope of God's purposes toward mankind, Paul's mind overleaps the bounds of history and time. With its center in Christ dwelling within the heart, his theology widens to embrace the entire created universe. The mystery of the gospel lay hidden in the world's foundation. The blood of the cross extends its reconciling virtue to "things in heaven" along with "things on earth" (Col. 1:20). Creation and redemption are parts of one design, with the Lord Christ supreme in both (Eph. 1:22, 23; Col. 1:14–20). The angelic powers are His subordinates and scholars, learning God's wisdom from the church (Eph. 3:10; Col. 2:10, 15). On the other side are ranged the hosts of Satan, ruling in the heathen world, against whom believers contend armed with "the full armor of God" (Eph. 2:2; 6:10–12). Thus the Christian system attains its full breadth and grandeur. Paul's theory comprehends the whole sum of things, and ranges through eternity. "For in Him [Christ] all the fulness of Deity dwells in bodily form" (Col. 2:9).

With the change of subject in the letters of the third group, we find a change in the manner and attitude of the writer. Colossians and Ephesians are transcendental and dogmatic, while Galatians and Romans are psychological and historical in their cast of thought. In the latter epistles we feel the force of Paul's logic; in the former we admire the breadth of his philosophy. There he sounds all the depths of the heart; here he soars to the farthest bounds of human thought.

But the apostle never loses himself in speculation. From these celestial heights he descends with new vigor and insight to the level of ordinary life. Colossians 3 and Ephesians 4—6 give a fuller representation of practical religion than any of the earlier epistles. The completed doctrine of Christ's Lordship and of the nature and destiny of the church, the new humanity that He has called into birth, furnish the basis for *a new Christian ethics*, whose import has not even yet been adequately realized. The relations of family and social life belong to the divine order, founded from eternity in Christ; they are under His guardianship, and have their counterpart and ideal in His spiritual kingdom. Thus the secular becomes sacred, the natural is affiliated to the supernatural (Col. 3:17). The light of heaven shines upon our daily walk on earth; the love of Christ sheds its influence over the world's strife and toil, dispels its dreariness, transforms its selfishness, cleanses its impurity, delivers it from folly and vanity, and makes it a garden of the Lord bringing forth "(the fruit of the light . . . in all goodness and righteousness and truth)" (Eph. 5:9). Nowhere is *the Christian temper* in its commingled elements and its effect on human behavior so perfectly described as in certain passages in these epistles. "Whatever is true, whatever is honorable, whatever

is right, whatever is pure, whatever is lovely, whatever is of good repute," those who have received Christ and His new life will "let [their]
mind[s] dwell on" and practice in the world, so "the God of peace shall
be with" them (Phil. 4:8, 9).

The epistle to the Philippians holds a singular place in this connection, serving incidentally to combine the characteristic points in
the teaching of each of the three previous groups, and, in a certain
sense, summing up the doctrinal development of the letters which
have preceded it: compare Philippians 3:20, 21 with 1 Thessalonians
1:10, 1 Corinthians 15:50–57; Philippians 3:3–10 with Galatians
2:14–21; and Philippians 2:5–11 with Colossians 1:15–22. The last
passage gives to Paul's doctrine of the Person of Christ its most finished and sublime expression, and sets it as the key-stone in the arch
of his theology.

We have found in the Alexandrine Jewish theology, through
which Greek philosophy first came into contact with the gospel, the
external cause which turned Paul's mind in the direction it takes in
the epistle to the Colossians. At the same time, the new doctrine of
the epistles of this period is a genuine outgrowth of his earlier teaching. It is due to the inevitable logic of his thought, guided by the Spirit
of God and compelled to make Christ "all things and in all."

The Pauline theology has now attained its full stature. As an organic structure it is complete. "And He put all things in subjection
under His [Christ's] feet"; He is filled with "the fullness of Him
[God] who fills all in all," and given in His fullness to the church, a
bride who shall be worthy of her Lord (Eph. 1:22, 23; 5:25, 26). Paul's
principle of the believer's union with Christ has expanded and built
up itself, till it fills the world and rises to heaven and eternity. What
more is there left for him to say? It remains that he should set his final
seal upon the teaching of his life, and commit the great charge to the
times to come. And this is what the Pastoral epistles do.

They rehearse his doctrines here and there, in balanced and finished sentences. They apply them in their collective force to the practice of religion and right behavior in the church. They dwell at
length on the character that befits her ministers, and on the opposite
qualities that marked the false teachers already beginning to infest her
communion. They insist on religious character as the church's vital
need, her seal and security in perilous times. Piety and virtue are the

flower and fruitage of the life hid with Christ in God, and it is on the safeguarding of these that Paul's last thoughts are spent. He has planted and tended the garden of the Lord: he must *fence* it from ravenous beasts. In "the mystery of *godliness*" he sums up all the glorious revelations of Christ he had received (1 Tim. 3:16), and the "goal of our instruction" of his ministry is "love from of a pure heart and a good conscience and a sincere faith" (1 Tim. 1:5). Such are the things which those who follow him must "teach and preach," guarding evermore the great "deposit" which Christ Jesus in His unspeakable grace committed first to himself, and which he had kept faithfully to the end.

The four groups of epistles we may now characterize, from the most general point of view, as being respectively, in their relation to the apostle's ministry: *missionary, evangelical, edificatory, valedictory;* in manner, *didactic, argumentative, contemplative, hortatory;* in matter, *eschatological, soteriological, Christological, ecclesiastical.*

The Growth of the Church

Church life and administration occupied Paul's mind increasingly as time went on and his ministry drew to its close. The letters to Timothy and Titus are in fact ecclesiastical epistles. They deal with the practical affairs of the church, as the Ephesian epistle sets forth its principles and spiritual basis. The first epistle to the Corinthians gives us a vivid picture of the manifold elements that entered into the life of a Pauline church. Other letters have thrown additional light on the subject. And yet, ample as the material seems to be, it is extremely difficult to delineate the features of primitive church organization, and to trace the steps by which it was developed in the apostolic age.

Paul's earliest letters were written "to the church of the Thessalonians in God the Father and the Lord Jesus Christ." Here the church seems to present a *congregational* aspect. It is constituted by the local assembly of believers, who are distinguished by their faith in "God the Father and the Lord Jesus Christ" from heathen and Jewish communities around them. When he writes to "the church of God which is at Corinth, with all the saints who are throughout Achaia," "to all who are beloved of God in Rome," or "to the saints and faithful brethren in Christ who are at Colossae," such expressions indicate

a detachment of the church from its local habitat; the transition is effected from the *congregational* to the *connectional*, or collective, idea
of its constitution. When, finally, in the epistle to the Ephesians, he
speaks of "the whole building being fitted together is growing into a
holy temple in the Lord" (Eph. 2:21), of "the body of Christ" to
which God gave Him for head who is His own fullness (Eph. 1:22, 23)
and in which there is to be "glory in the church and in Christ Jesus
to all generations forever and ever" (Eph. 3:21), we have attained to
the full conception of the church *catholic* and *ecumenical*.

As to government and the distribution of church-office, the references of earlier epistles are slight and not easy of explanation. It
seems likely that the apostle did not impose a uniform plan upon all
his churches. The Thessalonians had "presidents," "those who dili-
gently labor among you, and *have charge over* you in the Lord, and give
you instruction" (1 Thess. 5:12), whom they are to treat with affection and respect. The same expression is applied to "the elders who
rule [who *preside*] well" in 1 Timothy 5:17 (similarly in 1 Tim. 3:5). We
may safely identify the Thessalonian presiding officers with the order
of "elders" whom Paul and Barnabas "appoint[ed] . . . in every city"
in completing the work of their first mission in Asia Minor (Acts
14:23; cf. Titus 1:5). Such "elders" Paul, we may presume, was accustomed to appoint in each new church, to preside at its meetings
and take the spiritual and administrative direction of its affairs. At the
same time, it is not the officers specifically, but *the church at large,*
which the apostle addresses in regard to the case of discipline that
arose at Thessalonica, and it is by the vote and action of the whole
body that he requires the necessary censure to be inflicted (2 Thess.
3:6–15; cf. 1 Thess. 5:14, 15).

In 1 Corinthians 5 this disciplinary action and responsibility of the
body of the church are conspicuously evident. Peremptory as his
own judgment is in the case of the incestuous person, the assembly
must concur in the sentence and itself expel the culprit. He writes,
"For I, on my part, though absent in body but present in spirit, have
already judged him who has so committed this, as though I were present. In the name of the Lord Jesus, *when you are assembled, and I with
you in spirit,* with the power of our Lord Jesus . . . to deliver such a one
to Satan. . . . REMOVE THE WICKED MAN FROM AMONG YOURSELVES"
(1 Cor. 5:3–5, 13). Neither 1 nor 2 Corinthians makes any reference

to church officers, unless such reference be found in 1 Corinthians 16:15, 16, but this passage seems to express the apostle's wish that the Corinthians should put themselves in line with other churches ("that *you also* be in subjection to such men"), implying that "elders" had not been previously recognized. It is difficult to understand how the scenes of disorder indicated in 1 Corinthians 14 could have existed under regular presidency; in correcting this disorder Paul appeals to the body of the church, without alluding to any authority except his own. In 1 Corinthians 11:34 there may lie an intention, not hitherto fulfilled, to organize this church like others. It is significant that in 1 Corinthians 12:28 he enumerates among the things "God has appointed in the church" *helps* and *governments*, corresponding to the offices of *deacon* and *overseer* (or *elder*), as we find them in Philippians 1:1 and the Pastoral epistles, but these functions existed at Corinth in idea rather than in fact. This church exhibits the characteristic traits of a Greek democracy, its abundance of talent, its vivacity and public spirit, with its fatal levity, turbulence, and fractiousness.

In the epistle to the Galatians we find the first distinct reference to the "teachers," or "instructors" (same wd. as in Luke 1:4; Rom. 2:18; 1 Cor. 14:19: kindred to *catechists*), who played so important a part in the development of the early church. At Corinth powers of "teaching" and "prophecy" seem to have been diffused through the church, and not committed to any specially chosen individuals (1 Cor. 14:26–31). Up to the time of 1 Timothy 5:17 this office was distinct from that of the "elders": "ruling" and "teaching" might, or might not, belong to one and the same person. In organizing the young churches of Crete, Paul desires that these functions should be combined (Titus 1:5–9). In Ephesians 4:11 "pastors and teachers" are associated, but not necessarily identified.

Through the whole apostolic age there were "prophets," men who by their gift of inspiration, the highest gift of all (1 Cor. 14:39), were associated with the apostles as founders and spiritual leaders of the church (1 Cor. 12:28; Eph. 2:20; 3:5, etc.). They had, as prophets, no administrative charge, and not unfrequently traveled from one community to another (Acts 11:27; 15:22, 32; 21:10), belonging to the church at large rather than to the local society. Other miraculous gifts, of "healing," and of "tongues," were greatly valued, but stood in no particular relation to church office. The several functions we have enumerated are brought together as "gifts that differ according to the grace given to us" in Romans 12:6–8, but in general terms such as scarcely allow us to think of them as being at this time distributed upon a fixed and uniform plan of church organization.

In Ephesians 4:11 there is placed next to the "prophets" among Christ's gifts to His church an order of "evangelists," or messengers of the gospel; compare the instance of "Philip the evangelist" (Acts 6:5, 8; 21:8), and Timothy (2 Tim. 4:5). At an earlier time *apostle*, in its wider sense, had served this purpose, being a general designation for a *missionary preacher* (Acts 14:14, Barnabas and Paul; 1 Thess. 2:6, including Silas and Timothy; etc.). The apostles, prophets, and evangelists belonged to the church generally, while the "pastors and teachers" naturally held a local charge. From Acts 20:28 (cf. 1 Pet. 2:25) it seems clear that *pastor* and *overseer* (guardian) were equivalent in Paul's phraseology.

In Paul's address at Miletus the "overseer" first makes his appearance. Not without design did the apostle introduce this word in place of "elder." The latter was ambiguous, being a title of Jewish office, and it did not sufficiently indicate the duty that passed on to shepherds of Christ's flock. Along with the "overseers" the "deacons" come into view in the Pauline churches shortly after this (Phil. 1:1; 1 Tim. 3:8–13). As the church grew and its charitable cares multiplied, the presbyter-overseers required assistance in this work, and the example of Jerusalem supplied a precedent (Acts 6), which Paul would be glad to follow. When in the address of his letter to the Philippians he formally distinguishes the "overseers and deacons" from the body of the church, it is manifest that church office is put upon a regular and permanent footing and the distinction of clergy and laity, ministers and people, is definitely established.

The Pastoral epistles add nothing really new to this simple outline of church administration, but they serve to fill in its details. We gather from them that "laying on of hands" was the mode of appointment to office and special vocation in the church (1 Tim. 5:22; 4:14; 2 Tim. 1:6; cf. Acts 13:3). In Timothy's case "the presbytery" of Lystra (or Derbe?) shared with Paul in this function. The "elders" are subject to discipline, and Timothy has to examine charges that may be brought against some of them at Ephesus, acting in this as the apostle's delegate (1 Tim. 5:19–21; cf. Titus 1:5). The power to ordain and the power to suspend from office naturally go together. The directions of 1 Timothy 3:1–13 imply that Timothy, in the choice of elders and deacons, would act in concurrence with the judgment of the church; they lay down the qualifications necessary in persons elected, but do not specify who the electors are. This would be understood of itself. The self-governing power which we found the Thessalonian and Corinthian churches to have a few years before, cannot have been wanting in Ephesus. The local community had a principal voice in choosing its officers; Timothy's part would be that of advising and approving, and finally of presiding in the ordination of the elected.

The care of *widows* had now become an important part of church business (1 Tim. 5:3–16; cf. Acts 6). Provision was also made for the rearing of orphans, and the entertainment of strangers, so we gather from 1 Timothy 5:10 (cf. Heb. 13:2). These and similar works of charity, along with the provision made in cases of necessity for the temporal wants of the ministry (1 Tim. 5:17, 18; 2 Tim. 2:4, 6; cf. 1 Cor. 9:6–18, etc.), imply the existence of church funds and exact financial arrangements. Considerable sums of money passed through the hands of the local overseers and deacons. Hence it is specified, in regard to both orders, that they must be "free from the love of money" (1 Tim. 3:3, 8; Titus 1:7, 8).

The stress of Paul's valedictory charge lies upon the office of *teaching and preaching* in the church. "Preach the word": this is his last injunction and is urged upon Timothy with awful solemnity (2 Tim. 4:1–8). The word of God is "the sword of the Spirit," the great weapon of Christian warfare. By it error is to be combated and sin rebuked; by it the church is nourished in godliness, and souls are won for God. With Paul's departure, fidelity in this work becomes more than ever imperative upon his successors (2 Tim. 4:6), and it devolves on them to commit this same charge to faithful and competent men (2 Tim. 2:2). Here, indeed, there is an apostolical succession: in the transmission of the gospel message, in the heritage of "a spirit . . . of power and love and discipline" (2 Tim. 1:7). But it is a succession that has not flowed in the channel of ecclesiastical prescription. Of this grace the Spirit still "distribut[es] to each one individually," and to every community, "just as He wills" (1 Cor. 12:11).

No word is said anywhere in Paul's letters that connects the powers of the ministry specifically with the administration of the sacraments:

in 1 Corinthians 1:17 he protests for himself, "For Christ did not send me to baptize, but to preach the gospel." It is evident, nonetheless, that the rites of baptism and the Lord's supper were everywhere "received from the Lord" as the most cherished privileges of faith, emblems of the life of fellowship with Christ in its beginning and continuance, the visible seal of its hidden realities and pledge of its future manifestation (Rom. 6:1–11; 1 Cor. 10:16–22; 11:23–26, etc.). But it is the "word" that gives efficacy to the outward ordinance (Eph. 5:26).

As to the *mode* of public worship and sacramental observance, and as to *methods* of church government and administration, there is little in the Epistles to guide us. The mind of Paul was occupied with other things. Such forms as then existed he does not seem to have prescribed by way of legislative enactment and as matters of fixed rule, but rather to have allowed them to form themselves out of existing material and as circumstances required, himself guiding and correcting the process as it went on. The future was left unfettered. The life of the Spirit in the church remained free to fashion its outward dress according to its own needs and impulses as a growing spiritual organism. Mosaism had provided a complete church polity, finished and rigid in every detail; Christ and His apostles acted otherwise. That there should be the two sacraments, that there should be pastors and teachers, rule and discipline, mutual edification and subordination, that a thorough organization of the church's powers is necessary for the service of Christ and the work of the world's salvation, all this is abundantly evident, but for the concrete application of these principles and their embodiment in positive institutions the living church, under the guidance of the Holy Spirit, is responsible. Let the truth of the gospel, let the spirit and character of the Christian life be maintained, and these external matters will shape themselves aright. Though "there are varieties of gifts, but the same Spirit. And there are varieties of ministries, and the same Lord. And there are varieties of effects, but the same God who works all things in all persons" (1 Cor. 12:4–6).

Such is the conclusion that we draw from Paul's church policy, so far as it is manifest in the epistle, looking both at what they say and what they leave unsaid. Forms of ritual and forms of government are gradually transmuted, under the changing conditions of life; they change no less inevitably where the change is disguised, in churches which hold strictly to traditional and fixed rubrics. "But now abide faith, hope, love, these three" (1 Cor. 13:13), and where these are, there is the Spirit of the Father and of Christ. Such a church, one yet manifold, one temple of many buildings, the apostle Paul left behind him spread from Syria to Spain, witnessing everywhere that "grace of God has appeared, bringing salvation to all men" (Titus 2:11). This living church, of the living God, was the grand creation of the apostolic ministry. It was the counterpart and interpretation of the Pauline doctrine: "Built upon the foundation of the apostles and prophets, Christ Jesus Himself being the chief corner stone" (Eph. 2:20).

The Epistle to the Hebrews

In the early Greek manuscripts of the New Testament Paul's epistles form a distinct volume, entitled *The Apostle*. Within this volume the fourteen letters are named from the churches or individuals to whom they were addressed: *To the Galatians, To Philemon,* and so on. Similarly this epistle is entitled *To the Hebrews*. In the oldest copies it stands tenth in order, coming last of those addressed to churches. There is evidence that in some previous editions it had occupied a more prominent place, standing fifth (following Gal.), or even fourth (following 2 Cor.), and so last among the larger epistles. When, after long hesitation, the Western church in the fifth century admitted Hebrews into its New Testament canon, it was set last of all, being attached as a kind of appendix to the other thirteen, and we have received it in that position. The Syrian church, in its ancient version, also sets this epistle last of the fourteen. Luther, in the German Bible, separated it from the Pauline letters, and placed it after those of Peter and John.

In regard to the place of this epistle in the New Testament scriptures, East and West were at first divided. The scholars of the East, especially of Alexandria, recognized its inspiration and from this inferred its apostolic origin; the scholars of the West denied its apostolic origin, and therefore its inspiration and canonicity. But, as Bishop Westcott puts it:

> The spiritual insight of the East can be joined with the historical witness of the West. And if we hold that the judgment of the Spirit

makes itself felt through the consciousness of the Christian society, no book of the Bible is more completely recognized by universal consent as giving a divine view of the gospel, full of lessons for all time, than the epistle to the Hebrews.

Destination of the Epistle

The writing has neither address nor author's name. Its destination has been traditionally handed down, and is confirmed by the contents of the letter. It is needless to give detailed proof of this. At every point one is conscious of listening to the voice of a Jewish Christian pleading with his compatriots. The epistle is saturated with Old Testament thought. More than this, the community addressed is a *purely Jewish* one. The salvation of the heathen is never discussed (though it is implied in Heb. 2:9, and elsewhere), nor is a word said concerning the relation of Jews and Gentiles to each other in the church. So far as this writing is concerned, the Gentiles might have no existence. They are not excluded, and on the principles of the writer could not be: his theology is Pauline in its breadth. But they are out of sight. The church addressed appears to be wholly Jewish in its environment; its hopes and fears, temptations and trials are such as belonged to Jewish Christians living among their fellow Jews.

Such a community could hardly be found outside of Palestine. And the language of Hebrews 9:6–10; 10:1–22; 13:9–15 implies a familiarity with the sacrificial system and an attachment to it, such as Jews *of Jerusalem*, above all others, must have possessed and felt.[1] Hebrews 13:12–15 all but name the Holy City as the home of the writer and his readers: "Jesus . . . suffered *outside the gate*. Hence *let us go out* to Him outside the camp, bearing His reproach (cf. Heb. 12:2). For we do not have an lasting city, but we are seeking the city which is to come." Such words might, indeed, be addressed to Jews everywhere, to whom Jerusalem, whether far or near, was the one city of God, but they were calculated to appeal with their full force to men who lived within its walls, and who clung with all the affection and

---

1. The texts quoted to show the writer's ignorance of the ritual system of Jerusalem (Heb. 7:27; 9:4; 10:11), seem to us to bear another interpretation.

tenacity of their Hebrew nature to that "holy place of the tabernacle of the most High" whose existence had been the pride of their life and the foundation of their hopes. In this light, a pathetic force belongs to the example of the patriarchs, held up to men called to wander forth "seeking a country," in quest of "the city which has foundations" (Heb. 11:8–10, [14]), who knew well how Jesus had said that before long "not one stone" of their glorious temple "[would] be left upon another." What comfort there was for exiles from the beloved city in the thought that they had "come to Mount Zion and to the city of the living God, the heavenly Jerusalem!" (Heb. 12:22).

But if the readers were Jews of Palestine, and probably of Jerusalem, they were *Hellenistic Jews*. The author, who classes himself with those whom he addresses, thinks and writes in Greek. He is master of a finished and powerful Greek style. His Bible is the Septuagint; he shows little or no knowledge of the Hebrew text. His culture is Alexandrian and philosophical rather than rabbinical, although the roots of his doctrine are in Palestinian soil and he is free from the vicious allegorism of the Alexandrines. He uses the dialect of Philo and the Hellenistic Book of Wisdom. We venture to think, therefore, that the epistle was addressed not to the Judean church at large, but to the Hellenistic section of it, or, perhaps, to a particular circle within the Greco-Jewish communion at Jerusalem. Considering the intimate acquaintance the writer professes with his readers and their history as a church, and considering his promise to come and see them (Heb. 13:23), we cannot believe, as some do, that his homily was addressed to Hebrew Christians generally. It has a distinct community and a definite locality in view.

Among the "many thousands" of Christian believers, "all zealous for the Law," whom James pointed out to Paul at Jerusalem a few years before (Acts 21:20), there must have been a number of separate congregations; to one of which, consisting of Hellenists, this writer had formerly belonged. The barrier of language had from the first (Acts 6:1) distinguished the Greek-speaking Christians of Jerusalem from their brethren; of this important body the martyr Stephen, and probably Philip the Evangelist, were members. On the supposition that the readers belonged to the Hellenistic side of the Jerusalem church, we can account for the degree of wealth and liberality with which they are credited: see Acts 6:10; 10:34; 13:2, 5, 16. Elsewhere this church appears as a recipient, rather than a bestower, of charity. But among the Jews of foreign speech settled at Jerusalem there would be found men of substance, such as "Mnason of Cyprus," Paul's host in this city (Acts 21:16), who brought there the wealth acquired in other lands, and on their benevolence the poverty of their native brethren made great demands.

The title of the epistle has been urged against its Hellenistic destination, and it is true that in the New Testament "Hebrew" and "Hellenist" are used as antithetical terms (Acts 6:1; 22:2). But later Christian writers, at the time when this designation (*To the Hebrews*) first appears, called all the Jewish Christians "Hebrews," without distinction.

If the epistle were addressed, as we conjecture, to a limited community of believers in Jerusalem, and in the period preceding the fall of that city, when the mother church was decimated and dispersed and its traditions well-nigh destroyed, we can understand, better than on any other supposition, how the author's name has disappeared.

Date of the Epistle

This "word of exhortation" was written under the shadow of the doom of national Judaism. The signs which our Lord had given in His prophecies of judgment were being fulfilled, and "the day" was visibly approaching which He foretold (Heb. 10:25). The "forty years" of respite (A.D. 30–70) granted to unbelieving Israel, had nearly expired (Heb. 3:7–19). A "shaking" was going on in the powers of earth and heaven, among all the civil and religious institutions of the nation, which portended their speedy removal (Heb. 12:26–29). Judaism still exists; "but into the second [tabernacle] only the high priest enters, once a year," and "every priest stands daily ministering and offering time after time the same sacrifices, which can never take away sins" (Heb. 9:7; 10:11; cf. Heb. 8:4), but the entire system "is becoming obsolete and growing old [and] is ready to disappear" (Heb. 8:13).

For a generation Judaism and Christianity, the old covenant and the new, had subsisted side by side, but this could be no longer. "He takes away the first in order to establish the second" (Heb. 10:9). The supreme crisis has come for these Jewish Christians. They had clung to the ancient fold, and in their zeal for the Law (Acts 21:20) had strained their loyalty to Jesus Christ almost to the breaking point. Now they must choose between the two camps. Either they will follow their high priest "outside the camp, bearing" from their Jewish kinsmen "His reproach," or they must take sides with His enemies and crucifiers and remain within the gate of Jerusalem, awaiting the judgment of which "a certain terrifying expectation" filled every thoughtful Hebrew mind (Heb. 10:27, 37–39). This, they must understand, would be to "shrink back to destruction." The siege and fall of Jerusalem verified the warning in full measure.

The above indications point with emphasis to *the last days of Jerusalem* as the time and occasion of this writing (cf. James 5:1–5, 8, 9), but not, apparently, to the very last days. The storm is impending; it has not burst. Jerusalem is not yet "surrounded by armies" (Luke 21:20). The writer expects to be able to visit his friends, but he sees there is no time for delay (Heb. 13:19, 23).

The Jewish war broke out in autumn 66, and the siege of Jerusalem by Titus commenced early in A.D. 70. If we place the epistle near to the former of these dates, we are not far from the truth. In Hebrews 13:7 the Hebrews are bidden to be mindful of "those who led you, who spoke the word of God to you (cf. Heb. 2:3, 4); and considering the result of their conduct" to "imitate their faith." Now, James of Jerusalem died a martyr in A.D. 62, and Peter probably in 67. Allowing for these events, we are brought down to the year 67 as the earliest date for the epistle. With this the reference to Timothy in Hebrews 13:23 accords. Combining it with the words of 2 Timothy 4:9, 21, we are led to suppose that Timothy had obeyed Paul's summons to Rome, that he also had been imprisoned, and was now released after his master's death. We must admit that elements of conjecture enter into these calculations, but, on the whole, it seems tolerably certain that this work was written about the year A.D. 67, within a year or so of the Pastoral epistles, shortly after the death of James, Peter, and Paul, and two or three years before the fall of Jerusalem.

When the writer says, "Those from Italy greet you," it may either mean that he is writing *from Italy* and sends this message on behalf of the brethren there, or (more probably), that it comes from a party of Italian Christians, fugitives from their country, in whose society he finds himself.

Aim and Character of the Epistle

Judaism is on the eve of destruction. And yet, as it often proves with a falling cause, it exerted a marvelous energy and fascination in its decay. The dying flame of the nation's life blazed up from its socket with fierce heat, and Jerusalem for a time resisted the whole might of Rome, and held the world's amazed attention. The Jewish people were seething with excitement, with a passionate and contagious enthusiasm for their country and their faith. The days of the Maccabees and of David seem to have returned, the time that every patriotic Israelite prayed and longed for. The national flag is lifted against Rome, the new Edom and Babylon. It was the war of Jehovah, and woe to every traitor!

In the breast of the Hebrew Christians there was a distressing conflict. The influences around them all tended in one direction; the instincts of their Jewish blood, the courage and pride of their race, the entreaties and threats of their kinsfolk, joined with their own devout attachment to the forms of the old religion to create a stream playing upon them with immense force, whose pressure in a moment might carry them utterly away from their Christian moorings (Heb. 2:1). They had been faithful hitherto, but would they "hold fast the beginning of [their] assurance firm until the end" (Heb. 3:14)? To side with Judaism now would mean utter apostasy from Christ; it would signify nothing less than endorsing that they "crucify to themselves the Son of God," renouncing His sacrifice for sin and "regard[ing] as unclean the blood of the covenant"; it would be, in a word, to "trample under foot the Son of God." They would thus expose themselves, without a place for repentance, to the "consuming fire" of God's judicial anger (Heb. 3:12, 17; 4:11; 6:6; 10:26–31; 12:29). These fearful warnings, especially when coming from a writer so calm in temper and measured in style, imply that the danger of apostasy was real and urgent in the extreme.

The letter is written, therefore, *to dissuade Hebrew Christians from returning to Judaism.* This aim determines the course of its teaching throughout. The author desires to give his fellow-believers a true conception of the worth of Christianity. He would have them understand the all-sufficiency of Christ, the greatness and completeness of the salvation He confers (Heb. 2:3; 9:26–28), the transcendent excellence of the new covenant made in His blood (Heb. 8:6; 13:10), the glory and stability of the kingdom He has founded (Heb. 12:22–28), and "a great reward" which fidelity to Him will insure (Heb. 10:35). Realizing these things and "fixing our eyes on Jesus" from the fears and temptations that surround them, they will like Him be enabled to "endure the cross, despising the shame" (Heb. 12:2); they will bear the taunts of their kindred as His reproach; they will cheerfully leave behind them city and goods, content to belong to the heavenly Zion and to have in it "a better possession and an abiding one" (Heb. 10:34).

The new covenant is set forth, on the one hand, in contrast with the old, which was imperfect, transitory, and in process of dissolution, but at the same time as the *fulfillment* of that covenant, superseding the ancient religion because it realized its ideal and satisfied the spiritual needs which it created, abolishing it as the substance does the shadow, as the finished work the preliminary sketch and outline (see Heb. 8:5; 9:1–12, 23; 10:1–18; 12:18–24). Of this theory of development applied to the Mosaic system, Paul gives a hint in Colossians 2:17; it is the working out, in another direction, of his great maxim stated in 1 Corinthians 15:46: "However, the spiritual is not first, but the natural; then the spiritual."

In this line of argument, we perceive, the writer reproduces the mental process by which he himself has been brought to the knowledge of Christ. We can read, through this epistle, the spiritual biography of a typical Hebrew Christian, whose Israelitish faith has been gradually transformed by the spirit of the gospel.

> He speaks as one who, step by step, had read the fulfillment of the old covenant in the new, without any rude crisis of awakening or sharp struggle with traditional errors. His Judaism has been all along the Judaism of the prophets and not of the Pharisees, of the Old Testament and not of the schools (Westcott).

Judaism is here, above all, *the Levitical religion.* Aaron, rather than Moses, is its representative figure; the sanctuary, not the decalogue, is its center. It is viewed essentially as a system of worship, a means of approach to God; not as a system of law which men must keep in order to be just with God. The salvation of the gospel is set forth throughout in terms drawn from the ritual of the Pentateuch. Instead of the atonement and justification by faith, we read "cleanse your conscience from dead works to serve the living God," of men who "draw near with a sincere heart in full assurance of faith, having our hearts sprinkled *clean* from an evil conscience and our bodies washed with pure water" (Heb. 9:14; 10:22). The sacrifice of Christ and the Person of Christ are no less dominant in this than in the previous epistles, but they are viewed from another standpoint, and apprehended in a different way. In Hebrews the blood of Christ *cleanses worshipers;* in Romans it *reconciles enemies.* The powerful delineation of Christ's divine-human glory given us in the early chapters of this work, leads up to the conception of "the great high priest" standing within the veil, the intercessor and forerunner of His people: the Christology of the other epistles culminates in the thought of the "Lord Jesus" to whom "every knee should bow . . . and that every tongue should confess" (Phil. 2:10, 11) the "head over all things to the church" (Eph. 1:22) in whom it is God's purpose to gather into one the universe of being.

One cannot observe the salient features of this epistle without being sensible of the contrast it presents to the known letters of Paul. And yet there is very much in common. The epistolary method is the same, only pursued here more methodically. The topics treated are largely the same, both in doctrine (cf. Col. 1:14–22; 2:9, 10 with Heb. 1:1–4: Christ is in each case contrasted with *angels;* Phil. 2:5–11 with Heb. 2:8–10; Rom. 3:19–25 with Heb. 9:11–15), and morals (cf. Rom. 12:10–13; 1 Thess. 4:6 with Heb. 13:1–6; Gal. 6:6–10; 1 Thess. 5:12, 13 with Heb. 13:16, 17). The prayer of Hebrews 13:20, 21 we should not be surprised to find in one of Paul's epistles. Above all, the theology of the writer is of a truly Pauline stamp, both in the doctrines which compose it and in the proportion and emphasis with which they are delivered. The universal lordship and all-sufficiency of Christ, His nature equally divine and human, forgiveness and sanctification man's great necessities, the inadequacy and failure of Judaism to secure these ends, are truths as prominent in this epistle as in the others, and equally absorbing to the mind of the writer. The glory of Christ and the way of man's salvation occupy our thoughts in Hebrews as much as in Romans or Ephesians. We cannot wonder that Origen should say, "The thoughts belong to the apostle," and that the vast majority of readers have accepted this writing without any difficulty as the work of Paul.

But on closer examination there exhibits itself to us in this profound work *another mind*, the mind of one who had passed through the school of Paul and deeply imbibed his teaching, but who sees everything from his own point of view and in the light of an experience of another order than that of Saul the Pharisee, one who has worked over again and restated for himself and for his Hebrew brethren, under an inspiration peculiar to himself, the doctrine of the Gentile apostle. The fact that Hebrews has so much in common with other epistles makes the difference more impressive, and harder to explain on the theory of a single authorship. If the same subjects are treated, it is from a new standpoint; if the same phrases are used, it is always with an altered shade of meaning.

Moreover, there are some things that we have learned to think inseparable from Paul's teaching, which we miss in this epistle. This writer has not, so far as we can find, Paul's peculiar mystical sense of *the indwelling Christ*. The Lord Jesus Christ is our brother, helper, shepherd, priest, intercessor, Savior to the uttermost; it is impossible to exalt Him more highly, to trust and adore Him more perfectly than this great teacher does. But the thought of the believer's personal union with Christ, never absent in Paul, is absent from this epistle. The phrases *in Christ, in the Lord,* and the like, which Paul is in the habit of using whenever he speaks of Christian acts and states, are suddenly and completely dropped; not once in this long epistle does such an expression occur as *Christ in me,* or *in you.* Nor does the author once (in his genuine text) speak of the Redeemer as *Christ Jesus,* which Paul does constantly. Once the apostle, in 1 Timothy 2:5, calls Christ "one *mediator* also between God and men": this conception possesses the writer of Hebrews always. It is the thought of God, the *living God,* that fills his soul. Holy fellowship with God is for him the end and sum of life. "My soul thirsts for God, for the living God; When shall I come and appear before God?" (Ps. 42:2). Such was the need that had brought him to Christ. In Jesus He has found the way to this end, which Judaism pointed out and prepared for, but never reached. Christianity is to him the perfect religion, because it inaugurates the perfect and everlasting worship.

We observed at the outset how thoroughly in Paul *the style* and the man are one. It is no less the case here. One cannot describe the manner and temper of the author without opposing him to the apostle of the Gentiles.

> The style, the temperament, and the cast of thought characteristic of this epistle are markedly different from those traceable in the letters to the Galatian, Corinthian, and Roman churches. The contrast has its source in difference of mental constitution and of religious experience. Paul was of an impetuous, passionate, vehement nature; hence, his thought rushes on like a mountain torrent leaping over the rocks. The writer of our epistle is obviously a man of calm, contemplative, patient spirit, and hence the movement of his mind is like that of a stately river flowing through a plain. Their respective ways of looking at the law speak to an entirely different religious history (A. B. Bruce).

The style throughout, as Westcott well says, is that of "a practiced scholar." Here is nothing "unskilled in speech" (2 Cor. 11:6) anymore than in knowledge: no abrupt apostrophes and lively dialectics, no unfinished sentences, no marks of the unstudied conversational freedom with which Paul at once delights and tries us, and this in an epistle which affords abundant room for the exercise of these qualities of style, had the apostle himself been the writer.

> The calculated force of the periods is sharply distinguished from the impetuous eloquence of Paul. The author is never carried away by his thoughts. He has seen and measured all that he desires to convey to his readers before he begins to write. In writing, he has, like an artist, simply to give life to the model which he has already completely fashioned (Westcott).

We agree entirely with W. F. Moulton's judgment, expressed in his valuable commentary on this epistle[2]:

> From point to point the general likeness to Paul's writings comes out more and more plainly; on the other hand arises a continually increasing wonder that the Greek sentences and periods should ever have been attributed to that apostle's hand.

---

2. Published in the New Testament Commentary for English Readers, volume 3 (Cassells), and reprinted in a small and cheap volume (Titus—James) in the *School Commentary* (Cassells).

The Author of the Epistle

From what has been said, it is clear that we cannot acquiesce in the traditional belief that the apostle Paul wrote the epistle to the Hebrews.

The letter is strictly anonymous. The writer has nothing to say about himself, except that "we [himself included] are sure that we have a good conscience" and "desiring to conduct ourselves honorably in all things," that he is "convinced of better things" of his readers than some of his words seem to imply, that he has "written . . . briefly," and that he hopes through their prayers to "be restored to them the sooner" and will come to see them, if possible, in Timothy's company (Heb. 6:9; 13:18, 19, 22, 23). Not that he seeks to conceal himself; he is well known to his readers, and knows them well. But he is a modest man, full of his argument, full of the needs and the peril of those to whom he writes, and it does not occur to him to refer to himself more explicitly. (It is conceivable, however, that the original address has been, for some reason or other, suppressed.) His personality remains entirely in the shade. In Hebrews 2:3, 4 he distinguishes himself from the original disciples of the Lord, and takes his place along with his readers generally[3] among Christians of the second generation (contrast 1 Cor. 9:1; Gal. 1:1, 12, with Heb.).

The conclusions we have arrived at respecting the character of the epistle, the readers to whom it was addressed and the author's relations with them, seem to exclude the hypothesis of a *mediate* as well as that of the direct Pauline authorship. This, however, was not the view held by the earliest authorities upon the subject, the learned Greek fathers, Clement of Alexandria (A.D. 200) and Origen (A.D. 230). Clement declares that Paul wrote the epistle in Hebrew, and that Luke translated it for the use of the Greeks, and this notion seems to have been a generation older than Clement. Yet it cannot have been firmly established, for Origen, a generation later, who was the greatest scholar

---

3. This may seem to militate against our supposition that the readers were Christians of Palestine, and probably of Jerusalem. For there would be living in the Holy Land so late as A.D. 67 not a few who had seen the Lord Jesus on earth. Still, the bulk of the Hebrew Christians at this time were believers at second-hand, and this would be the case especially with Hellenists of Jerusalem, of whom many had, in all probability, migrated there from abroad.

of his time, tacitly rejects it. Judging the hypothesis of translation by internal evidence, "we do not hesitate to say that it is absolutely untenable" (Moulton).

Origen writes thus:

> If I were to express my own opinion, I should say that the thoughts are the thoughts of the apostle, but the language and the composition those of one who recalled from memory and, as it were, made notes of what was said by his master. If, therefore, any church hold this epistle as Paul's let it be approved for this also, for it was not without reason that the men of old times have handed it down as Paul's. But who wrote the epistle, *God only knows certainly*. The account that we have received is twofold: some say that Clement, who became bishop of Rome, wrote the epistle; others that Luke wrote it, who wrote the Gospel and Acts. But on this I will say no more.

The hypothesis of a Hebrew original has disappeared. And it is clear that already the name of the author was lost, and the men of Origen's time had no more certain means of ascertaining it than ourselves. Notwithstanding this uncertainty, Origen speaks of *"fourteen* epistles of Paul," and quotes this writing habitually under the apostle's name. Authorship was evidently understood with some latitude. Delitzsch has powerfully advocated the theory of Origen, inferring *Luke's* literary authorship from the resemblances between Hebrews and this Evangelist's writings.

Jerome and Augustine, guided by Origen and the Greek fathers, persuaded the Latin church in the beginning of the fifth century to accept the epistle. Jerome writes: "The custom of the Latins does not receive it among the canonical Scriptures as Paul's." Henceforward the custom changed.[4] The writing was known and valued in the West from the beginning; Clement of Rome (about A.D. 100) makes use of it. Tertullian of North Africa, contemporary with the Alexandrian Clement, calls it the "epistle of Barnabas," and gives it a secondary authority; there are traces of the same tradition in Jerome, and elsewhere. This view has been revived of late, and commands a large vote among modern scholars. Barnabas was a Hellenistic Jew, but con-

---

4.   But it was on canonicity rather than authorship that Jerome and Augustine insisted; on the latter point they did not go further than Origen, if so far.

nected with the church of Jerusalem by family ties and residence (Acts 4:36, 37; 11:22; Col. 4:10). At the same time, he was an associate of Paul, and a man of kindred type. His surname, conferred by the apostles, signifies "Son of Encouragement" (Acts 4:36), and our author describes his letter as a "word of exhortation" (Heb. 13:22). Moreover, Barnabas was a *Levite, and* this is the sacerdotal epistle, which makes Christ, above all things, the "high priest of our confession." To the Barnabas hypothesis Renan inclined; also B. Weiss and Salmon, doubtfully. On the other side, we must remember that the writer appears to include himself in the younger generation of believers (Heb. 2:3, 13:7), whereas Barnabas was a contemporary of the first apostles, and as we gather from his position in Acts 11—15, especially from Acts 14:12, was considerably senior to Paul.

At the Reformation the old controversy respecting this epistle revived. Erasmus writes: "Paul, or whoever was the author of this epistle." Calvin, though he calls it "apostolical" and attributes the doubts of its authority to "the artifice of Satan," yet continues: "For my part, I cannot be brought to recognize Paul as the author." He sees, too, that it is no translation from the Hebrew. "The writer professes himself, in the second chapter, one of the disciples of the apostles," but "*who* he was makes little matter": so Calvin concludes.

Luther started a new theory. He put the writing down to *Apollos.* Apollos is described in Acts 18:24 as "a certain Jew, . . . an eloquent man," and "mighty in the Scriptures," and our unknown author was all this. He was an "Alexandrian by birth," and this would account for the Alexandrine features of the epistle. He was closely connected with Paul, and regarded by him as one who built on the foundation he had laid and "watered" what he had "planted" (1 Cor. 3:5–10); this is very much the relationship of the fourteenth to the earlier epistles. Luther's bold conjecture has been endorsed, more or less positively, by such critics as Bleek, Lünemann, Kurtz, Alford, Farrar, and Moulton. The chief objection to this view, besides the silence of ancient writers, is that Apollos labored in the field of the Gentile mission. His Christian course began at Ephesus about A.D. 52; we find him next at Corinth in A.D. 55 or 56, and hear of him in Crete about A.D. 66 (Titus 3:13). There seems to have been no opportunity for his acquiring the early and close acquaintance with members of the church in Palestine which the epistle implies. If it could be shown that the letter was addressed to *Alexandria* (as Farrar thinks) rather than Jerusalem, the case would be altered.

One other possible candidate is suggested for the authorship: "May not the author have been *Silas?*" Godet has asked. Riehm and B. Weiss have shown in how many respects this church-founder and apostolic man meets the conditions of the case. Silas (or Silvanus) was a leading member and "a prophet" in the church of Jerusalem (Acts 15:22, 27, 40). His Roman name and citizenship, besides his association with Paul, mark him out as a Hellenist. He was Paul's associate for two years on his second missionary journey, and must have been imbued with Pauline doctrine. During the same period Timothy was his comrade, to whom this author refers in Hebrews 13:23. He acted as Peter's secretary in writing his first epistle (1 Pet. 5:12, 13), and there are distinct points of connection between Hebrews and 1 Peter. If, in 1 Peter, as seems likely, "Babylon" signifies Rome, then Silas was in Rome, associated with Paul, Luke, and Timothy, shortly before the date which we have assigned to this writing, and we can account for the resemblances of language which connect together Hebrews, the Pastoral epistles, and the writings of Luke. As a younger colleague of apostles, Silas could naturally speak in the language of Hebrews 2:3. But neither his name, nor that of Apollos, is ever mentioned by antiquity in this connection.

On the whole, we conclude that the epistle was written by Silas, or Barnabas, or *someone connected with Palestine among the many inspired men of the second Christian generation* who are unknown to us. Our ignorance of the person of the writer in no way diminishes the value of this Scripture; nay, it should rather, as Westcott says, "enlarge our sense of the spiritual wealth of the apostolic age." If it should be found that "a noble picture, which had been attributed to Raphael, was not by that artist, there would not be one masterpiece the less, but *one great master the more*" (Thiersch).

ADDITIONAL NOTE: Harnack has advanced the hypothesis that the epistle was addressed by *Priscilla and Aquila* (observe the "we" of authorship) to the Christian circle meeting in their house at *Rome* (see Rom. 16:5); Professor Peake (in the *Century Bible*) leans to this view. Von Soden (*Encyclopedia Biblica*), McGiffert (*History of Christianity in Apostolic Age*), Weizsäcker (*History of Apostolic Age*), maintain vigorously, but unconvincingly, a *Gentile* destination for the writing.

Analysis of Hebrews

This work is more regular in structure and rhetorical in form than any previous epistle. Romans resembles it in logical development, but it is less of a formal treatise than this. With great homiletical skill the writer interweaves his exhortations with his teaching, taking advantage of the practical points of his exposition as they arise. From the beginning to Hebrews 10:18, however, the epistle is chiefly *doctrinal*; from that point to the end, almost wholly *hortatory*.

The central doctrine is that of the high priesthood of Jesus Christ: "We have a great high priest who has passed through the heavens, Jesus the Son of God" (Heb. 4:14). Its fundamental Old Testament text is Psalm 110:4, so often quoted: "The LORD has sworn and will not change His mind, 'Thou art a priest forever, According to the order of Melchizedek.' "

A. THE DOCTRINE falls into two main divisions: (1) concerning *Christ the Mediator* of the new covenant, Hebrews 1—7; (2) concerning *the new covenant* and its efficacy, Hebrews 8:1—10:18. More briefly: (1) the Priest, (2) the Sanctuary.

THE PRIESTLY OFFICE AND WORK OF JESUS CHRIST

I. Concerning Christ Himself, Hebrews 1—7

§ 1. In His *Person* (Heb. 1, 2):

(a) As *God's Son* and *the Heir of all things* (Heb. 1).
(b) As *Jesus, the brother* of God's saints (Heb. 2:5–18).

In both these respects He is compared with *angels*, to whom on the divine side He was absolutely superior, though as man "for a little while [made] lower" (Heb. 2:7): in the exhortation that follows, He is compared in a similar strain with *Moses* and with *Joshua*.

The doctrine of § 1 (*a*) is improved in (α) the brief homily of Hebrews 2:1–4, bidding the readers *not be carried away*, and of §1 (*a*) and (*b*) together, in (β) the exhortation of Hebrews 3 and 4 based on the history of the "good news" (Heb. 4:2) of Israel's original call, which bids them *hold fast their confidence to the end*.

Hebrews 4:14–16 sums up the foregoing sections, and is the starting point for that which follows.

§ 2. Concerning Christ in His *priestly office*, for which by all that has been said before He is shown to be supremely qualified: Hebrews 4:14—7:28, "*Such an high priest* became us" (Heb. 7:26, KJV).

Here we distinguish:

(a) His *appointment by God*, in which He *resembled Aaron*, Hebrews 5:4–10;

(b) His *correspondence to Melchizedek*, the Old Testament type of a perfect priest, by which He *surpassed and superseded the Aaronic order* (Heb. 7:1–28), especially in these two points, namely, that Christ's priesthood was inherent in His person and unlimited in duration, and that it was "according to the power of *an indestructible life*" (Heb. 7:16). Hence it was the subject of a solemn *oath* on God's part (Heb. 7:20–25).

Here lies the pith of the epistle, that which will tax the intelligence of the readers, but the doctrine which, if they grasp it, will break the spell of Judaism for them. So the writer prefaces this part of his argument with a third and full homily (γ), exhorting them to *go on to perfection* (Heb. 5:11—6:20).

II. Concerning the new covenant, Hebrews 8:1—10:18.

§ 1. A new and better covenant there must be, Hebrews 8, for:

(a) *Christ's priesthood implies this*, Hebrews 8:1–6 (cf. Heb. 7:12), and

(b) *the old covenant* was essentially *defective*, as Scripture shows, Hebrews 8:7–13 (cf. Heb. 7:18, 19).

§ 2. The new covenant compared with the old, in its sanctuary, sacrifices, and so forth, Hebrews 9.

(a) Differing as the *worldly, carnal,* and *temporal* from the *heavenly, spiritual,* and *eternal,* Hebrews 9:1–15;

(b) but *blood-shedding*, the sacrifice of life, is common to both, Hebrews 9:16–22.

(c) Differing as the *passing shadows* from the *one abiding substance* of salvation, Hebrews 9:23–28.

§ 3. The religious perfection imparted by the new covenant, Hebrews 10:1–18.

By its *perfect sacrifice*, a sacrifice performed by *the will* of the victim (Heb. 10:5–10), *full remission of sins* is secured, which involves everything else.

Here the argument culminates: "For by one offering He has perfected for all time those who are sanctified" (Heb. 10:14; cf. Heb. 7:25). Our perfect Priest, presenting in "the greater and more perfect tabernacle" His perfect sacrifice, has now *a perfect holiness* to impart to us.

B. The Exhortation extends from this point nearly to the end, Hebrews 10:19—13:17. Three considerable homilies (α, β, γ) have been already interjected, so that the hortatory quite balances the doctrinal part of the epistle. These practical paragraphs are continuous in thought, though separated in place. They are carried forward as follows:

(δ) He exhorts the readers to *faithfulness to the new covenant*, Hebrews 10:19–39:

(a) in the *right use of its privileges*, Hebrews 10:19–25;

(b) in fear of the *consequences of apostasy*, Hebrews 10:26–31 (cf. Heb. 6:4–8);

(c) in recollection of *their former endurance*, Hebrews 10:32–39.

(ε) He encourages them by *the history of the heroes of faith*, the "many sons" of Hebrews 2:10 (cf. Heb. 6:12), crowned by *the example of Jesus*, Hebrews 11:1—12:4.

(ζ) He at once consoles them by the thought of *their sonship, proved by chastening*, and warns them of *possible disinheritance*, Hebrews 12:5–17.

(η) He enforces all this, finally, by a vivid presentation of *the glory and permanency of the new kingdom of God*, to which they belong, Hebrews 12:18–29.

Hebrews 13:1–17 consists of general exhortations, in the midst of which:

(θ) the writer urges his readers to *a final rupture with Judaism*, Hebrews 13:10–14.

The epistle concludes with the Paul-like prayer of Hebrews 13:20, 21, marked however with the distinctive token of *the blood of an eternal covenant*, and with the personal notes of Hebrews 13:18, 19, 22–24, which give it the character of a letter.

It is sealed with the Pauline benediction, Hebrews 13:25, with which this little book may also close:

GRACE BE WITH YOU ALL. AMEN.

Postscript: Locality of Paul's "Galatia"

Sir W. M. Ramsay, in his very valuable and original work on the *church in the Roman Empire* (3d ed., pp. 8–11, 61–66, 74–111), contests the prevailing view, on which we have proceeded in chapters 4 and 7, as to the locality of Paul's "Galatians." The force and ability of his argument, and the wealth of local knowledge which he brings to bear upon it, compel a reconsideration of the matter. He has proved that Pisidian Antioch, Iconium, Lystra and Derbe, the cities evangelized by Barnabas and Paul on the first recorded missionary tour of the latter, lay within the bounds of the province of Galatia as it then existed; that the apostle was accustomed to use the Roman provincial titles, and that the one common name by which the dwellers in these cities could be addressed, and would probably prefer to be addressed, was "Galatians," although they were not of Galatian race. These South Galatian cities lay on or near the chief route of land-traffic and the highway of the gospel from east to west (Syrian Antioch to Ephesus), along the main track of the apostle's missionary career; whereas North Galatia, the district of the native Galatae, was comparatively secluded and difficult of access. Even if Paul had gone so far out of his way, churches founded here could not, it is argued, have possessed the importance to his mind which these communities have, on the showing of the epistle, and their establishment is ignored in the narrative of Acts. The illness which occasioned Paul's preaching to the Galatians (Gal. 4:13), befell him, as Ramsay imagines, in Pamphylia on the first tour in Asia Minor,

171

obliging him to travel inland from the malarious coast of Perga to Pisidian Antioch: Acts 13:14 states the bare fact, without the reason. The word "Galatian" (only the adj., not the n. *Galatia*) occurs but twice, cursorily used, in Acts (Acts 16:6; 18:23), and the expressions of Luke—"the Phrygian and Galatian country," "the Galatian country and Phrygia (or Phrygian)"—denote, as R. contends, not two associated districts, but *one* district known by two names, the region at once Phrygian (ethnically) and Galatian (politically), of which Antioch was the capital, namely, South-western Galatia. The above are the main points in Professor Ramsay's theory.

The following considerations tell against it:

1. *The language of Acts 16:6.* This statement (see NAS), which is no recapitulation of Acts 16:4, 5 as Ramsay would have it, on the face of it points to "the Phrygian and Galatian region" as a new region of travel distinct from that traversed in Acts 16:1–5, to which the missionaries proceeded because they were "forbidden by the Holy Spirit to speak the word in Asia." If this "Phrygian and Galatian region" was not the district around Antioch, long ago evangelized, it could only be the country lying north and northeast of this, where the highlands inhabited by the old Phrygian population stretched to and overlapped the borders of Galatia proper. Under the Roman government surely some passable road existed from Antioch, "the governing and military center of the southern half of the vast province of Galatia" (Ramsay 25), to Ancyra its capital city. Acts 16:6 indicates that Paul at this point was driven out of his intended course (along the Ephesian trade-route), and Galatians 4:13 implies as much: the different reasons assigned are not contradictory; they apply perhaps successively.

2. *The connection of Galatians with Romans.* Sir W. M. Ramsay is obliged to date the Galatian epistle earlier than the third missionary journey, for the apostle, when he wrote it, had only been *twice* among his readers (Gal. 1:9; 4:13), whereas at the outset of the third journey he traversed South Galatia (Acts 18:23: on Ramsay's hypothesis) for a third time. Ramsay thus places an interval of two years, on his own showing (but it was something more like four years), between Galatians and Romans, ranging the former in the first group of epistles, with 1 and 2 Thessalonians, instead of the second. But if internal evidence proves anything, it proves that Galatians and Romans are neighbor

epistles, the offspring of one birth in the writer's mind. Lightfoot's conclusion, that Galatians comes between 2 Corinthians and Romans, will not be easily set aside. See chapter 4 above, and pages 114–118.

3. *The relations of Barnabas to South Galatia.* Barnabas was the joint-founder with Paul of the churches of South Galatia, which were established on the mission related in Acts 13, 14. But in the epistle Paul claims an unshared and unqualified authority over his Galatians. He refers thrice to Barnabas by name (once in terms of condemnation, Gal. 2:13), but appears quite unaware of any relationship between his old companion and the readers, and he is in no way embarrassed by the fact that Barnabas, to whom the South Galatian churches owed allegiance equally with himself, had differed from him on the grave questions at issue in the epistle. Now Paul was particularly sensitive on this point, and speaks elsewhere of those who are "overextending" and "build upon another man's foundation" (Rom. 15:20; 1 Cor. 4:14–16; 2 Cor. 10:13–16) with a contempt some measure of which would fall on himself, if he really ignored Barnabas' paternal rights and interest in the churches of the first missionary tour and elbowed him out of the partnership, as he must have done on the South Galatian hypothesis. The language of Galatians 2:1, 4, 5, 9, 10, implies that Paul and Barnabas stood together, in the eyes of the church, as colleagues in the direction of the Gentile mission, so far as it extended up to the date of the Council at Jerusalem. The fact that the southern churches were not under Paul's special and independent jurisdiction explains his scanty reference to them. See only 2 Timothy 3:11; they are possibly included in 1 Corinthians 16:1.

4. South Galatia was, as Ramsay has proved, a district of greater importance in the first century than the country of the native Galatians, and its churches played a larger part in the propagation of the gospel than those of the outlying northern district. This is probably the reason why the former, and not the latter, are conspicuous in Acts. But *why should Paul have written his letters only to churches of the first rank,* or felt the warmest affection for those that lay along great highroads? Colossae was a second-rate provincial town, but the visit of Epaphras, and the ominous heresy which he reported as arising there, drew from the apostle one of the most profound of his writings. The kindness lavished by the Galatians on Paul had touched his heart, and abundantly justifies his distress at their perversion. Besides,

North Galatia was not an unimportant region. Ancyra, its capital, was the head of a vast province, and would be the fittest center for the diffusion of Christianity through the midland and north of Asia Minor. To have reached Pontus so soon as is indicated in 1 Peter 1:1, the gospel must have traveled to North Galatian early in the apostolic age.

5. When Paul was stopped by a divine admonition (Acts 16:6) on the confines of the province of Asia, he would naturally gravitate towards the capital of the province whose southern border he had now twice traversed. It was *his practice to make for the chief city* of each Roman "diocese" in which he labored. Unless, moreover, the apostle had at some time previously broken ground north of the Syrian high-road and put the gospel in the way of reaching the whole of Asia Minor, he seems to boast too much when he writes to the Romans (Rom. 15:19), "so that from Jerusalem and round about as far as Illyricum I have *fully preached* the gospel of Christ."

6. If as the epistle to the Galatians gives us reason to apprehend, the defection of the churches of (North) Galatia continued and this region was lost to the Pauline mission, such defection would be an additional *reason for Luke's passing over this field almost in silence.* He does not in the least pretend to give a complete and uniform account of Paul's missionary career. What do we know of the "noble" church of Beroea, of the churches, of Cilicia, or of the churches of the Gentile mission in Syria outside of Antioch? It is possible to press too far the correspondence between Acts and the Pauline Epistles.

See further on this question the writer's article on *Paul* in Hastings' *Dictionary of the Bible*, volume 3, and on the other side, Ramsay's *Paul the Traveler and Roman Citizen*.

Index

See Table of Contents for other, principal headings.